Straight Talk *with* POST-OP & A DOC

Firm, Fair & Fun Answers to Your Questions
About Living Fully in Recovery From Obesity
After Weight Loss Surgery

by

CARI DE LA CRUZ *and*
CONNIE STAPLETON, Ph.D.

Publisher's Note

Published by

Mind Body Health Services, Inc.
www.mindbodyhealthservices.com

ISBN: 978-1497350441

Library of Congress
Control Number: 2014905361

Printed in the USA

DEDICATION

This book is dedicated to anyone who ever struggled with the "whys" of obesity and wants to get "wise" about living fully in **Recovery from Obesity.**

ACKNOWLEDGMENT

THE POST-OP SAYS: To my (sexy) husband and number one supporter, Juan De La Cruz (aka MexiKen)–Thank you for loving me and believing I could become the woman you knew I was born to be. When God brought us together 26 years ago, I had no idea where we would journey, but I'm grateful we traveled together. You are an amazing man, husband and father. I love and adore you more everyday, and I'm joyful to be your wife. | To our daughter, Hannah– You've become an extraordinary young woman, exceeding even my wildest imaginings (and believe me, they were pretty wild!) You are courageous, creative, witty, bold, intuitive, brilliant, unstoppable and beautiful. Thank you for your honesty and willingness to do the hard work so our family can live and love fully in Recovery. I am blessed to be your mama. | To my own mama, Carol Worth, for always believing I could do anything I wanted to do with my life and for seeing the things I couldn't see in myself. Your unconditional love showed me how to love others with God's love, and your commitment to daddy for nearly 50 years showed me how to love for a lifetime. Thank you for your courage, resilience, compassion... and crocheting. As Pop would say: I love you to pieces. | To my big brother, Greg (the unwitting source for much of this book): 1) I'm okay with the fact that my friends only liked me because they thought you were cute, and 2) I don't blame you for that whole "sorority" thing; I didn't like them, anyway. | Finally, The Doc, who gave me her acknowledgment *after* I'd already written mine so, I'll look rude if I don't say *something* to her: *Thanks a lot, Doc.**

Okay, there's much more about The Doc in my Recovery Story at the end...I promise.

ACKNOWLEDGMENT

THE DOC SAYS: My greatest thanks for this book go to The Post-Op, Ms. Cari De La Cruz (with <u>three</u> last names). Cari is my business partner, but she is so much more. She is my friend–a friend in the truest, deepest sense of that word. We work together, laugh together, cry together, struggle together, have MUCH fun together, and do some pretty awesome creating of Recovery information together! Thank you, friend, for all of that! I am a much better person for our work together and our friendship. The book, like all of our projects, has been fun–and frustrating, at times, as well! But damn, friend, we work well together! | As with everything I do, I thank the Lovebug, who remains calm and patient when I do not. He loves me, and for that, I am eternally grateful. And I LOVE my Lovebug! | And to my family (to include the Lovebug, of course), who is my greatest source of joy and with whom I treasure every minute, I am beyond grateful for. They support me, encourage me, and love me and have been part of this professional journey every step of the way. | Lastly, to everyone who has walked, and who is walking, the road of Recovery, I thank you for being part of showing me and the world how to live fully. Recovery is a gift, without which, I would never have co-authored this book, or done anything as a psychologist–because I wouldn't have been one! God has blessed me in so many ways. Sharing Recovery with others is my way of giving back–and I'm grateful to ***be doing so with Cari!***"

APOD

ACKNOWLEDGMENT

APOD SAYS: To those who have supported us and championed our work throughout the years...those who join us on our monthly APODCast...those who come to hear us speak at conferences and bariatric practices...those who participate on our Facebook page, and ALL who have shared what you have learned with your friends: We are humbly grateful for your support and encouraged by your willingess to work on your Head, Heart and Health to live fully in Recovery From Obesity.

**We know we can't do this alone –
and we *certainly* can't do it without you!**

TABLE OF CONTENTS

Cari De La Cruz & Connie Stapleton, Ph.D.

INTRODUCTION

WHY did we write this book?

The short answer is, *"Why NOT?"* The longer answer is: ***Because you ASKED for it***–and–we figured it would be great to share our answers in one, convenient place. Oh, and it's hard to highlight important things on a Facebook Wall. Here's the deal, after weight loss surgery, some post-ops get *"wise,"* while others simply get more *"whys"*:

> *"Why am I still struggling with my weight?"*
> *"Why am I hungry?"*
> *"Why can't I reach my goal?"*
> *"Why aren't I happy?"*
> *"Why am I so afraid I'll regain all of my weight?"*
> *"Why do I still feel fat?"*
> *"Why didn't the surgery work for me?"*

i

Left unanswered, these profoundly confounding questions can undo the benefits gained from improved health and mobility, keep a person from living fully in Recovery from Obesity, and lead right back to a life of unhealthy thoughts and behaviors. In our nearly twenty years of combined experience working in this growing community of shrinking people, we've learned that after surgery, many post-ops end up questioning their decision to have weight loss surgery (WLS) because they feel more vulnerable, insecure, fearful and uncertain than they did before surgery. Ultimately, they lose weight and gain unhappiness, which all too frequently translates into the dreaded regain!

This profusion of confusion is precisely why we wrote this book. After all, who better to answer the tough questions than a Doc who knows "WHY" so many people become obese and a Post-Op who knows "HOW" it feels to be obese? You get the best of all worlds, rolled into one firm, fair, fun package.

Okay, WHY...Straight Talk?

We don't *sugar coat anything (sugar coating is what got you here in the first place).*
We do *give it to you firm and fair (with a bit of fun thrown in for good measure).*
We will *hold you accountable and encourage you to be responsible.*
We are *living what we say, not perfectly, but with continued effort–every single day.*

WHY...A Post-Op & A Doc?

Here's what we say in all of our official brochures: *"A Post-Op & A Doc (APOD) is a surprisingly obvious synergistic pairing of Cari De La Cruz (a bariatric post-op) and Dr. Connie Stapleton (a psychologist specializing in recovery and weight management). Together we guide people in a firm and fun way, beyond a life focused on the scale, to living fully in recovery from obesity...because we believe it's good to know, and even better to understand."*

What that means is: *Together, we have the education and experience to help others learn to get what they say they want from weight loss surgery – improved health and a better quality of life. We just happen to call that, Recovery from Obesity.*

Okay, but WHY...Recovery From Obesity?

Well, obesity is a chronic and debilitating disease and, since people recover from diseases all the time, why shouldn't they live fully in Recovery From Obesity?

How is the book organized?

Before you go scanning the table of contents for chapter names, you should know that this book is divided into twenty-two sections, where each section features our answers to your question. Since you don't have to read it cover to cover, if you're feeling a bit rebellious, you can start at the end, skip to the middle, then thumb through the pages and pick the question nearest where your thumb ends up! However you find your question, we do suggest you read both answers from The Post-Op and The Doc, do the HoMEWork that follows, then tidy up with the thought-provoking quote at the end! Since it's organized by question, it's super easy-to-read when you only have a few minutes to spare (or just need a break from Facebook).

Whether you read a question a day or a question a week, we hope you'll begin applying what you learn right away (then, share your stories of growth with us!) Why? Because we love to hear about how you've overcome the challenges that fed your obesity and paved the road to your recovery! Oh, and besides…we need stuff for our next book!

Now: Time to get "wise" while we answer your "whys"!

WHY…Should I read this book?

▶ IF you want what you say you want (improved health, quality of life, and a little bit of peace) and you aren't doing what you said you would do to get it, *then this book is for you.*

▶ IF you want more out of your post-op life, *then this book is for you.*

▶ IF you're dealing with regain, *then this book is for you.*

▶ IF you're not living the life you expected after WLS, *then this book is for you.*

▶ IF you feel like a failure, haven't reached your goal weight, didn't stay at your goal weight, reached your goal weight…and just aren't happy, *then this book is for you.*

▶ IF you want to live fully in **Recovery From Obesity**, *then this book is for you.*

READ IT.

Q

"I recently heard someone talking about their 'inner critic' and their 'inner cheerleader.' I hear from my inner critic all the time! What do I need to do to turn down the volume of the critic so I can better hear the voice of my inner cheerleader?"

Cari De La Cruz & Connie Stapleton, Ph.D.

THE POST-OP SAYS

I don't know about you, but I have more voices in my head telling me what I "should" and "shouldn't do" than the Mormon Tabernacle Choir! The only problem is, mine aren't making beautiful music in four-part harmony, and…they're all ME. So, how do I drown out the endless chorus of voices that criticize, nitpick and undermine my recovery from obesity? How do I silence the sour notes of negativity and turn up the volume on the sweet songs of success? The short answer is, I don't. Surprised? Well, let me change metaphors on you to better explain this.

When I first began therapy, I brought this exact "problem" to my counselor and asked him how to control the noise and stop all of the conversations in my head. I explained that I kept hearing all sorts of negative thoughts and they were drowning out all of the positive messages I was trying to have. I told him I wanted to stop the bad stuff and only hear the good stuff – at which point, he shared a very wise tale about a barrel of monkeys…well, a brain full of monkeys, actually.

Evidently, there is a well-known condition, which The Buddha referred to as "Monkey Mind." In this parable of simians, the student learns that we all have chattering monkeys racing around in our brains. They are in constant motion and generally don't shut up for a moment's peace. Interestingly, in the tale, we learn that one of the "louder" monkeys is fear. Yup, the "fearful monkey" screeches the loudest. So, not wanting to be drowned out, the other monkeys screech…even louder.

And so it goes – until we do something to tame the monkeys. Notice I didn't say "shut them up?" That is because the goal is to calm the monkey chatter– not silence it– through things like meditation, purposeful breathing and relaxation.

Now, the original question was about shushing the "critical" monkey to better hear the "cheerleader" monkey. Similar to another parable about fighting wolves, the easiest answer is, the one you feed (or listen to, in this case), is the one that will prevail.

So, the best way to shut down the negative monkey is to feed (encourage) the positive monkey with whatever positive message it is that you want to hear. If you want to quiet fear so you can hear courage, or quiet anger so you can listen to happiness, first calm yourself (i.e., get yourself to a peaceful place). Then, you can tune-in to the monkeys that are saying things you want to hear. I mean, think about it -- if you're in a giant football stadium, surrounded by screaming fans, can you really hear the person sitting next to you? Same idea…

So, back to the monkeys: I have a monkey that loves to criticize me by saying things like, "See that person over there? They don't like you and they're saying mean things about you to other people so they won't like you either!" Just typing that made my "confident" monkey fall right off the jungle gym. Okay, he fell because he was pushed by the "mean" monkey – but I let it happen by not giving the confident monkey what he needed to stay solidly put. I didn't listen to him. If I want to change that, I need to ignore the mean monkey and pay attention to the confident monkey because he has something important to tell me. He is saying (quietly, I might add), "It's true. Some people don't like you, but you don't have control over their thoughts. You are who you are and sometimes people won't like you. Your job is to be true to yourself and not intentionally do harm. Don't do things to try to make people like you. Be accountable to who you are and you will soon find others who share your beliefs and like to be with you." Those are very nice words, but I never heard them before because I kept listening to the mean monkey.

3

Now let's talk about *your* monkeys. The critical monkey is saying, "*You're still fat. You've lost weight, but you still look fat. Look at all of that hanging skin. Look at those flabby arms. You look older now that your face is thinner and doesn't have fat to fill in the wrinkles…*" Shut up, monkey! Instead of listening and putting our energy here, let's feed the cheerleader monkey instead.

First of all, I'm going to inhale deeply…hold it for a bit…then exhale slowly. I might have to do this a few times until my heart stops racing! Now I'm going to listen for the other monkey…Hmmm….I think I hear a whisper…"*It's true that I have extra skin now, but no one sees that under my clothes; I can dress to draw attention to the areas of my body I like. As for my face wrinkles? Well, I'm not getting any younger, and in the end, I'd rather be healthier and look older and thinner than fatter and younger!*"

That's weird. I've never heard those thoughts before. What's different now? Oh, I decided to ignore the critical monkey and focus on the cheerleader monkey!

"Gimme a 'C!' Gimme an 'A!' Gimme an 'R!' Gimme an 'I!' What's that spell? YAY FOR ME!"

Which monkey are you going to feed? Which monkey deserves your attention? In the noisy chorus of monkeys in your mind, which monkey is singing the song you want to hear? Hey, when I don't like a song on the radio I change the channel. If you don't like the songs you're hearing, change the channel until you hear a monkey melody that you can sing along with.

4

There are many different ways to think about the "inner critic." There are also probably a lot of different ways to work on turning down the inner critic and increasing the volume of the inner cheerleader...which I'll get to in a moment. Naturally, I am going to talk about where the voices of your inner critic originated. This may or may not be important to you when you go about working on making the change from "critic" to "cheerleader," although I've noticed that a lot of people are interested in understanding why they have an inner critic in the first place.

Consider this a mini-lesson in child development–in this case we're talking about you when you were a child! Remember that children don't understand verbal language when they are born. The first way we begin to develop our self-esteem is from the non-verbal feedback we get from others. The "others" we have access to in our first years of life are primarily our family members, or the people who care for us most of the time.

If our caretakers give us positive non-verbal feedback most of the time (smiles, laughter, cuddling, cooing, playing, etc.) then the message we get from them is that we are "good," that we bring joy to others, that we please those upon whom we are dependent. Positive non-verbal feedback leads to a positive sense of self. If our caregivers are stressed, are chronically ill, unhappy with others in their lives, active in addiction, or otherwise pre-occupied, we may get mixed non-verbal messages–sometimes they are engaged and interact with us in positive ways (smiles, hugs, baby-talk)–and other times, they show their frustrations with their situations or with other people when they interact with us (have an angry tone, frown, cry, fail to interact when feeding or changing us). This can cause uncertainty about our self-worth, as we can only gauge our worth by the reflections we get from others during those very first years.

If our primary caregivers are mostly unhappy in their own lives, their relationships, or their jobs, OR if they have poor health and don't feel well most of the time, they may be in a negative mood most of time. If this is the case, they may be grumpy or sad or angry or preoccupied when they interact with us. Because we are just babies, we don't know that they are upset with their boss, their significant other, or upset because of their finances or their health. We just know they aren't smiling and laughing and playing when they feed us, change us, bathe us, and put us to bed. Infants and toddlers don't have the ability to think, "Gee, Mom is crying and it's because she had a fight with Dad," or "Wow! Daddy must have had a bad day at the office. He sure is grumpy tonight." Little people only know that Mommy is sad and Daddy is mad and therefore "I," the child, don't make them happy.

Like it or not, that's child development. So–although you may not remember this time in your life–your parents' moods and behaviors had a huge impact on your very early self-development. As did those of whomever else took care of you when you were teeny tots.

What's that got to do with the "inner critic" or "inner cheerleader?" You can probably guess this part. The more positive the interactions that others had with you, the greater you feel about yourself and the louder your "inner cheerleader" will be versus your "inner critic."

But wait–there's more! Just like the infomercials! As we get older we learn to understand language, as well as various tones of voice. If we are regularly criticized, then, yep–our self-esteem is damaged and the voice of the "inner critic" grows louder. Criticism from parents, teachers, coaches, Scout leaders, relatives, and yes, friends and peers, all impact our sense of self. If you're told you'll "never amount to anything," "aren't smart enough," "don't have what it takes," "are fat," "are lazy," "aren't enough like your brother or sister," etc. then your self-esteem is damaged. BY THE WORDS OF OTHER PEOPLE! Why? Because if the people saying these things to us matter to us (and most of them do, particularly when we're young), then we internalize these messages. In other words, we believe them. And the "inner critic" is born… we start saying those very same things to ourselves.

People with high self-esteem usually had a lot of positive affirmation from other people. They were encouraged, they were told they "could" try things, they were told they were good at things and that it was okay to be who they were. (No one–hopefully–is told they are good at everything, but people with positive self-esteem were definitely given more praise and encouragement than discouragement.)

Now, before you get defensive about your parents and how encouraging they were, remember, it may have been other people who discouraged you, who maybe teased you or picked on you. Self-esteem develops in a number of ways. So, I'm not blaming your parents!

Back to the "inner critic" and "cheerleader." Here's the real problem. When children internalize (start to believe and then say to themselves) the negative messages they have heard from others, they grow and develop that inner critic, which is why we say we are "our own worst enemies." For most of us, as we get older, people stop criticizing us, (at least to our faces). I KNOW…there are a lot of strangers who do make rude and inappropriate comments to people who are overweight. I'm not saying it doesn't happen. I am saying, however, that as adults, we do most of the damage to ourselves. We reinforce negative messages we got earlier in our lives…"I'll never succeed at…," or "I don't know why I bother," or "What's the use…" or "I can't do…," or "I'm a loser," or any number of negative self-statements. This is our inner critic.

How do we change that? Like most other things:
1) we become aware that we do it,
2) then we choose what we want to do about it.

We can choose to continue the negative self-talk (which is really just another way of saying we can choose to retain our "inner critic".) We can, alternately, decide that the critic is not helping us be the person we want to be and therefore choose to change how we talk to ourselves. We can also accept the fact that the "inner critic" lives on inside, acknowledge it as a nuisance, and go about living a full life in spite of it.

Is it that simple? Yes, it is. Is it easy? Not a chance. You have years and years of hearing, repeating and believing the negative comments about yourself. You have likely perfected the art of self-criticism. You can't change this until you are aware that you are doing it.

How do you become aware of your negative self-talk (stinkin' thinkin')? You listen for it. You ask your friends to point out to you when you say something negative about yourself out loud.

Then what?

Then, you make a conscious choice to change that negative statement to a more positive one. "I can't do that," becomes "I'm going to put some effort into that and see what I can do." If you hear yourself saying, "What's the use in trying? I'll never be able to do this," then force yourself to change it to something like, "This is hard! I'm going to do this differently this time. I think I can make some progress." AND, in the process, accept that you may not be able to STOP the automatic negative thoughts, but you can choose to realize they are there (which doesn't mean you like the thoughts or that you accept the negative thoughts as facts), and you go about making the wisest choice for yourself in the current situation, no matter what it is.

What if it doesn't work? It DOES work…if you work hard enough at it for long enough!

8

For one day, literally write down every negative thing you think to yourself about yourself. Next, write down a more positive alternative and work to use that version in your future self-talk! Repeat exercise as necessary (which may be for a very long time)!

....

9

HoMEWork = Work I do at HOME for ME.

ATTITUDE

" YOU MUST START WITH A POSITIVE ATTITUDE
OR YOU WILL SURELY END WITHOUT ONE. "

– CARRIE LATET, EIU

Q

" I thought I would like my body so much better after I lost weight following WLS. I've lost over 100 pounds… and now I like my body less! I know I can't be alone in thinking this.

How can I fix this? "

11

THE POST-OP SAYS

You just never know what's going to happen when you ask me a question. Half the fun is wondering what I'll say, but the other half is knowing that I might have some questions of my own before I can answer yours... which is odd, because I won't know your answers before I give mine, meaning you'll know mine, and I won't know yours. Hmmm...I wonder if knowing your answers would change mine? (*Hint*: Probably not, but isn't this fun?)

So, here goes:

1. Did you like your body when you were obese?
2. If you were not always obese, did you like your body when you were thinner?

Did you answer "Yes" to either of those questions? If you did:

3. What did you like most about it?
4. What did you like least about it?

If you never liked your body before WLS, choose one thing you liked the very *least;* If you said there was a time when you liked your body (or a part of your body), what part was it? I'm hoping you were able to find at least something you liked (even if it was your baby toe) because I need you to remember that "feeling" you felt about your body (or body part).

More questions:

5. Did you like it because you liked how you looked when it was uncovered/naked?
6. Did you like how you looked in certain clothing?
7. Did you like how you looked to someone you were romantically interested in?
8. Did you like the way you looked because you felt like everyone else looked the same way?
9. Did you like it because no one else looked as good as you?

Why am I asking all of these questions? Well, it's because I want you to be thinking about a time *other than this moment* so we can get to the heart of the matter. I want you to remember what it felt like *before today*. If you said there was never a time in your life when you liked your body, was it because you didn't like how you looked:

- Naked?
- Clothed?
- Compared to others?
- To someone you were attracted to?

Did I make you think? Good! Now, let's get back to the original question about why you don't like your body and how you can fix it! But, before we do: **More questions!**

Is it possible that you thought you'd like your body better after WLS because you thought/hoped it would look:

- Different than it does?
- Like you looked before?
- Like a super model with ripped abs and shapely legs?
- Like someone half your age (or maybe how you looked when you were younger)?

To me, all of these questions (and your original question) boil down to two things: **Expectations** and **beliefs**. Ask yourself: Before surgery, what were your expectations for how you would look after surgery? Did you have an image in your mind, maybe a picture of another post-op? Did you believe you were attractive before surgery? Were your expectations about how you would look after surgery realistic? Did your beliefs about your attractiveness change? Phew! Big questions for such a little book, don't you think?

Okay, since I don't know how you answered your questions, it's time for me to answer them from my own experience: I was not obese until I turned 24. I was overweight and out of shape–usually by about twenty pounds. In other words, I wasn't fat. The problem was, I had a *fat head*– and that means the person staring back at me from the mirror or the photograph wasn't the person I truly was. I *believed* I was fat, so no amount of coaxing or encouragement to the contrary could change that.

I was a bottomless pit of disappointment (and who could fill that up)? So, if I had unrealistic **expectations** before WLS, then…how could surgery fix them? It was pretty clear that unless I changed my thinking, I'd end up with a fat head on a smaller body!

Wanna know the first thing I learned about my fat head? The fat was all in my head! As it turns out, how I saw myself (my body) was directly connected to my *beliefs* about myself (and evidently there was a lot of "fat" between my beliefs and myself! But—wait a minute—you might be thinking, "Heh! That's not me! I didn't think I was fat, so I didn't have a fat head. I think I'll skip this question!"

Uh, not so fast, you see this fat head "fenomenon" doesn't just apply to someone who thinks they're fatter/bigger than they are, because even if you are obese, but don't see yourself as being obese (or never did), it's not much different than being thin and seeing yourself as obese. Was that as confusing to read as it was to write? Let me say it a little better: *Whether you saw yourself bigger than you really were or smaller than you really were, you didn't see reality in the reflection…you saw what you chose to believe.*

Hard to believe? Don't worry, it just means you're gonna need to fix your head if you want to accept your fixed body, and the first step in doing *that* is **accepting reality**. Believe me, my reality ain't pretty! I have "shrinkles" (wrinkles you shrink out of) on my "shrinkles"; my butt disappeared into my thighs (so, I have a thutt), and before reconstructive surgery, I didn't have arms, I had mud flaps, and my breasts were…well… let's just say in a police line-up, I'd have been arrested.

What's that you say? It's not fair because I had reconstructive surgery? Well, stick with me here, because it will soon make sense. At about one year post-op, I had lost just about all of my fat and was left with a surplus of dangly skin. When I looked in the mirror, I saw a Sharpei, but in pictures, I saw something completely different: I saw a slim, attractive woman. Yes, you read that correctly: *I saw a slim, attractive woman.*

Now, that didn't just "happen"—I worked hard at it. I exercised regularly and intensely; I spent time buying clothes that complemented my body (I didn't just buy clothes that "fit.") I spent time (and money!) with a make-up specialist, so I could enhance my best features (and take attention off the things I disliked). Oh, and I started therapy.

The important thing to understand is, before I made any changes to my new (and not-so-improved body), I had to learn to accept how my body looked. You got it–I had to face reality. The next step was working to improve the things over which I had *some influence*. I say "some influence" for a lot of reasons, including cost (how much money would I have to pay to fix everything I wanted to change?), time (how much recovery time would be required? Did I have enough vacation time?), and significance (in the grand scheme of things, how important was the work I was considering?) Part of that improvement was having reconstructive surgery. Before I could even determine that, I had to go visit some surgeons and get some estimates. Talk about sticker shock– once I had those costs and specifics spelled out in front of me, I began to adjust what I believed was important. Even then, I wasn't sure I could afford the surgery, so before I even considered it, I made a promise to myself that if things didn't work out financially, I would *accept* my arms and breasts as they were. Notice I didn't say I would *love* them? In my book (or, at least my half of the book) this whole process of acceptance, adjusting beliefs about ourselves, and realigning our expectations is not about **loving** stuff that isn't exactly "lovable" (apologies to all who preach that we must *love our bodies*). This whole question of disappointment in your body is about **accepting** the realities of the stuff that isn't exactly lovable. Guess what? That puts us squarely back in the realm of "head and heart stuff"...which is precisely where The Doc and my therapist(s) came in!

So, back to your question: You asked if you were alone in not liking your body since your weight loss and you asked how you could "fix it." Clearly, (as evidenced by my story), you are not alone and, while I can't fix your body, I sure can give you some pointers that worked for me to fix my fat head!

Now, way back in the beginning I asked you to remember a feeling you had about your body or a part of your body that you "liked." Do you remember that? No? Okay, I'll give you a few moments to recall...Ready? Start by looking at some pictures of yourself (before and after your weight loss). Objectively assess the changes (I suggest you write them down, but

15

that's up to you). If you have pictures of yourself standing next to people who haven't changed very much, see how different you look beside them. Note any similarities in yourself. You can do this exercise in the mirror, as well, although you won't have your old self for comparison (and there probably won't be anyone standing next to you...as a matter of fact, do this alone–ha ha.) The goal is to characterize (not criticize) what you see. *"My eyes are brown, I have a mole on my cheek, my hair is (natural) red..."* and so on.

Get it? Now, ask yourself, "Do I still *'like that thing'* about my body that I said I liked before? Do I think I can learn to *accept* more things about my new body than I was able to *accept* before? Is there anything about my new body I can *learn* to like (not love)?

Struggling? Let me help you: Maybe you can see your eyes better because your cheeks don't swallow them up when you smile (yes, that was my problem!) Maybe you only see one chin now, instead of three! Maybe you are able to wear pants without drawstrings–which means your clothes fit you better! Now, what if there are still some things you don't like seeing? I say, fix what's fixable–accentuate the positive and minimize the less-positive; clothe your body as it IS, not as you wish it were; strengthen your muscles under that extra skin, and when you're done, take a moment to *believe* that you are far better now than you were at 100 pounds heavier. In other words, change what you can change and change how you think about how you have changed!

This is not easy–especially if you *never* accepted yourself as you were. It takes time and practice, but consistency is the key. The more you do it, the better you'll become at it.

Remember, we aren't lingerie models (there are only about a dozen of those in the world, and even *they* don't look like super models without Photoshop!) We are normal people who wear normal undergarments–okay, maybe you wear those famous undergarments, but no one expects you to model them in the next catalog!

Am I in love with the body I have now? Yes and no. Yes, because I am happy it is smaller and looks good in clothing. No, because I have no business wearing shorts (even though I want to). Yes, because my remodeled arms look great in sleeveless clothes. No, because I have a neck like a turtle.

Yes, because I can cover my neck with a turtleneck. Are you getting the picture? You may decide that even though your legs or arms are saggy, wearing shorts or tank tops isn't a deal breaker.

This is a personal choice and no one can tell you how to feel about yourself.

THE DOC SAYS

O verweight and obese people often feel ashamed about, and dislike, their bodies. Interestingly, the vast majority of post-ops who have lost their excess weight, continue to struggle with body image issues.

Dr. Thomas Cash, author of The Body Image Workbook says, *"Body image refers to how you personally experience your embodiment. More than a mental picture of what you look like, your body image consists of your personal relationship with your body—encompassing your perceptions, beliefs, thoughts, feelings and actions that pertain to your physical appearance. Often a poor body image lowers self-esteem. Poor self-esteem means feeling inadequate as a person; it means you have low self-worth and don't highly value yourself. As much as one-third of your self-esteem is related to how positive or negative your body image is. If you don't like your body, it's difficult to like the person who lives there—you!"*

Wow, that's powerful! And true! Let me repeat that last line: ***If you don't like your body, it's difficult to like the person who lives there—you!***

Listen as I describe a person with negative body image versus a person with positive body image. Which best describes how you have felt about your body in the past, how you currently feel about your body, **and** how you want to feel about your body in the future?

The **National Eating Disorders Association** says that people with a negative body image "have a distorted perception of their shape, are convinced that only other people are attractive, feel ashamed, feel self-conscious, are anxious about their body, and feel uncomfortable in their body. The group further states that people with negative body image have a greater likelihood of developing an eating disorder and are more likely to suffer from feelings of depression, isolation, low self-esteem, and to be obsessed with weight loss."

On the other hand, the organization describes persons with a positive body image as "having a true perception of their shape, appreciating their body's natural shape and understanding that a person's physical appearance says very little about their character and value as a person; they refuse to spend an unreasonable amount of time worrying about food, weight, and calories; and they feel comfortable and confident in their body."

WOW! A person with a positive, healthy body image understands that their physical appearance does not represent their character. Said differently, the number on the scale does not tell you or anyone else if you have integrity, compassion, or anything else about your person! AND, more importantly, the definition of a person with a healthy, positive, body image refuses…yes **refuses**…to spend an unreasonable amount of time worrying about food, weight, and calories. Sadly, these are the exact things so many post-ops **continue** to focus on (the scale, calories, recipes, the Food Network, etc.)…and how they continue to hold themselves hostage to the disease of obesity.

On it's website, The National Eating Disorders Association states: "We all may have our days when we feel awkward or uncomfortable in our bodies, but the key to developing positive body image is to recognize and respect our natural shape and learn to overpower those negative thoughts and feelings with positive, affirming, and accepting ones." Note the focus on replacing negative thoughts with positive thoughts, and remember–this leads to positive feelings and behaviors. Changing your thinking requires consistent effort, but with practice, you can do this. You learned to speak, to walk, to ride a bicycle, to drive a car, and to do many other difficult things. You can do this, too–if you choose to. With continued **effort**!

Although your body changes rapidly after weight loss surgery, your body **image** doesn't improve that easily. You've got to work on improving your body image if you are going to keep your weight off. Patients often tell me things like, "Even though I lost 170 pounds after surgery and got down to 138 pounds, I still thought of myself as a fat person. I continued to feel fat and told myself my body was still ugly. I remained very self-conscious about my weight and shape. It seemed like I had gone through the surgery and all the work it took to lose the weight only to remain ashamed of how I looked. I focus on the extra skin I now have and the wrinkles on my face I didn't notice when I was heavier."

Two of my favorite words related to life after weight loss surgery: **acceptance and effort**. You'll need to accept that after weight loss surgery, you will have *some* extra skin…maybe *a lot* of extra skin. Some people may have expectations that after losing their excess weight, they'll magically have the skin tone of a 20-year-old athlete. Regardless of one's weight, when you're over "a certain age," as they say, your skin is going to age! Be realistic with regard to your expectations about what your skin will look like after you lose your excess weight. **Accept** that there will be some extra skin and, as I said, there may be *a lot* of excess skin. As some commercial on television says, "Love the skin you're in!" When you get sad that you have saggy skin on your legs, think, "I'm so grateful I can walk so much more easily in my saggy-skinned legs now that I've lost so much weight!" When you see the shrinkles on your abdomen (shrinkles are what post-ops call the wrinkles left after they shrink)–think to yourself, "This extra skin on my belly won't kill me, but that excess weight surely would have!" It's all a matter of how you choose to think.

And remember, as Cari noted, it doesn't mean you need to **like** everything about your body! You also don't have to let some unease about how you feel or look stop you from living the kind of life you want to live. Say to yourself, *"Come on, loose skin and healthier body–we're going bike riding. This is something fun we couldn't do before losing weight!"* Stop restricting your life because of unpleasasnt thoughts, memories or feelings. Take them with you and get out there and enjoy life!

MAINTAIN AN ATTITUDE OF GRATITUDE!

Dr. Thomas Cash, who wrote *The Body Image Workbook*, said, *"People who need to lose weight to improve their health should separate the goals of weight loss and body acceptance."* What a great point! You chose to have weight loss surgery to improve your health, save your life, and to have a better quality of life. Rejoice in having done that! Accept that extra skin is a reminder of being alive and healthy.

Make a list of things that your body can do now that you have lost excess weight that it couldn't do before you had weight loss surgery. Reflect on the joys of these things and read this list daily if necessary!

HAPPINESS

" HAPPINESS IS NOT BY CHANCE, BUT BY CHOICE. "

– JIM ROHN, EIU

Q

"Before I had gastric bypass, I would frequently 'sneak eat.' In other words, I wouldn't let others see me eating unhealthy foods in large quantities. I didn't think I would do this after surgery, but I still do!

Why do I do this and how do I stop?"

THE POST-OP SAYS...

I wish I could tell you that surgery magically fixes all of your thoughts, feelings, behaviors, and relationships...but it doesn't. What surgery does do is provide a powerful tool that can allow you to focus on changing your thoughts, feelings, behaviors and relationships–while losing weight and (hopefully) getting healthier. In my experience as a post-op, when we are not so fixated on the crushing day-to-day realities of moving and living, we're free to focus on all of the things we couldn't think about when we didn't have a tool like WLS. If you're like most obese people, before surgery, all of your thoughts were consumed (in one way or another) by food...your feelings about food...your thoughts about food...how you behaved around food...oh, and your relationship with food–which, as I mentioned–didn't change because of surgery.

About now, you're probably thinking, "I had surgery, and I can't eat as much a I used to, so why am I still consumed by my thoughts, feelings, behaviors and relationship with food? Here's your answer: Because surgery doesn't address any of that stuff...it simply makes it more possible for YOU to address it–and it sounds to me like it's time for YOU to address it!

Since I'm not a Doc, I can only answer this as a Post-Op who had a lifetime of experience at being sneaky with her food. It probably started in a very innocent way (like trying to hide my peas under my dinner plate because I didn't want to eat them, or filching an extra fig cookie when my mom wasn't looking), but it soon became a full-blown behavior! Now, you should know that my mom was pretty firm about not eating before dinner, because she said it would spoil my appetite. You know...come to think of it, "spoiling" your appetite should mean over-indulging not under-indulging, but I don't make the rules, so let's go with it. Mom said don't eat before dinner, so that was the rule. Which only meant that if I was going to break the rules, I'd have to do it where she couldn't see it...like at the corner drugstore where they sold my very favorite candy: *The Marathon Bar*. For the uninitiated, The Marathon Bar is made of chocolate that is magically "braided" (for additional strength) and stuffed with unbelievably gooey caramel. When you combine the two ingredients together, you end up with a substance that is so impervious to chewing it should be added to the Elemental Table (Mb2). Now, the amazing thing is, the magical Marathon Bar only cost $0.13–but lasted a really long time; it even had a ruler printed on the back of the wrapper, just to prove how long it would last.

Why am I describing this candy bar? (Stick with me, there's a reason... there's always a reason): One particular afternoon, at 4:30 PM, I set out to covertly break my mom's rules and "spoil" my dinner with The Marathon Bar. I had 30 minutes until dinner and the store was a scant five-minute bike ride from home. Lucky for me, I made good time, got there in four, swiftly bought the bar and quickly began to hide the evidence by eating it, when I encountered a little problem. Did I mention I'd recently gotten my braces off and now had an upper retainer? Did I mention that food could (sometimes) manage to find its way into the area between the roof of the mouth and the top of said retainer? Did I mention the other-worldly chemical composition of The Marathon Bar when chewed? I guess I forgot some of that, but you have to understand...this event happened a really long time ago, and even though I can now comfortably refer it as "one of those experiments I did in the name of science"–back then was a little closer to "things I unsuccessfully hide from my mom–who will ground me forever if she learns what I did."

But back to the increasingly desperate situation at hand (I remind you of the current state-of-affairs surrounding the clock): I started this sly adventure 30 minutes before dinner, took a 4-minute bike ride to the store, stood in line for 1-minute, spent 1.5 seconds ripping open the candy wrapper and was now 60-terrifying seconds into the first bite. Inexplicably–and I don't know how this happened–the chocolate and caramel had mysteriously and terrifyingly transmogrified into something akin to quickset concrete–though slightly more tasty. This left me with a mere 15 minutes to figure out how to pry the retainer from my mouth (without breaking it or pulling teeth) and hide the evidence of my devious act before dinner. Did I mention my mother's preternatural sense of smell with regard to chocolate? Did I mention she'd won awards for being able to lock onto the scent of a 1 pound box of candy at 100 meters? Try living with that when you have a brother who is a Type 1 diabetic. But back to my rapidly deteriorating sneak-eating

25

situation: After about 10 minutes of finessing and canoodling, I shifted into more aggressive tugging and wrenching, yet that blasted retainer remained securely soldered to the roof of my mouth with a chocolate weld so strong, it would take a blow-torch and a putty knife to break the bond. With five minutes to go until dinner, I decided my fate was inevitable and, despite my logic that eating the rest of the bar would somehow cause the seal to break between my mouth and orthodontic device–I rode the long, 4-minutes home, arriving just in time for mom to say, "Dinner's on! Wash your hands and come to the table!" Well, I successfully made it to the bathroom (ostensibly to wash my hands) where I spent the next two minutes attempting to dislodge my retainer with some mouthwash, toothpaste and peroxide–all to no avail. I was out of options.

"…..*Mom? Can you come here? I need your help.*"

Oddly, I cannot recall exactly what my mom said, but I can remember in vivid detail exactly how I felt: Ashamed, deceitful, confused, and cheated. That last emotion was because I felt betrayed by my orthodontist who had saddled me with this draconian torture device and was the source of my trouble. Funny how I wanted to blame others for my choices, but I was 13…what did I know?

Fast forward a few decades–okay, three–and I've learned (in no particular order) that it was time to stop blaming The Marathon Bar, my orthodontist, my slow bike and my mom and start facing the truth about my unhealthy relationship with food. Why didn't I change 30 years ago? Wasn't getting caught and punished enough motivation to change my behavior? If anything, getting caught simply made me more resolute in my efforts to hide food. "Next time," I declared, "I will remove my retainer first."

That wasn't quite the lesson…but hear me out: What does a chocolate bar have to do with you sneaking food? Regardless of your orthodontic history or choice of unhealthy snacks, you and I share the same problem: We both had a sick relationship with food and it didn't change just because we got caught or had surgery.

Here's the deal: If you want to stop sneak-eating, you'll have to face your relationship with food head-on, and that's going to require awareness, acceptance, commitment, attitude, accountability and effort, along with group support, therapy, and maybe even a program like Overeaters Anonymous. In other words, the sneak-eating is not going to change until you change it. The good news is you've figured out that, surgery didn't cure your obesity—so now, it's time to get help and start treating it.

27

THE DOC SAYS...

One of the questions I ask people during their pre-surgical psych evaluation is, "What makes you think having surgery will change _____?" In the case of the person asking this question, the blank is "eating unhealthy foods in large quantities." For others, "the thing" they hope/think/pray having weight loss surgery will include is standing at the refrigerator and mindlessly eating, their nightly ritual with half a gallon of ice cream, the "habit" of picking up food on the way home at a fast-food burger & fries joint, staying up after everyone has gone to bed to enjoy some alone time with their favorite treats, and snacking all day at work while on the computer.

I am a firm believer in weight loss surgery as a means to lose weight quickly in order to improve health and obtain quick weight loss results with the assumption that the first year will lead to engaging in healthy eating and exercise behaviors that will continue after "the honeymoon" is over. I work extremely hard to make that point clear a number of times in the time I spend with patients and state it over and over in the pre-surgery videos they are required to watch.

Alas, years and decades of unhealthy food-related habits, many which started out as important coping skills, and the lack of insight into the "purposes" that food serves, often leads to sometimes immediate resuming of unhealthy habits and unhealthy food choices. Hence, the very real need for the work that Cari and I, as well as many others throughout the nation and world are doing to work with post-ops to help them dig into their emotional relationships with food and life, rather than run from them with the same unhealthy food habits and/or the acquisition of equally unhealthy behaviors of other sorts (alcohol, shopping, food network, etc.).

There IS no "easier or softer way," as they say in the 12-step recovery world. Owning the truth, learning to understand how food helped avoid unwanted thoughts, feelings, bodily sensations (anxiety, depression, etc.), memories, and learning healthier ways to deal with life "on life's terms," (meaning dealing with whatever the reality is at the time, to include difficult thoughts, feelings, sensations and memories).

You have to choose. I like to use this picture…Imagine, if you will, that you are standing on the edge of a huge, very wide pond. You can barely see that there is a world on the other side. Where you live (in your obesity) has some very nice aspects. Yet, the overall picture has become drab. There seems little hope for life to improve in drastic ways on this side of the lake. Drastic changes are necessary in order to live longer, live healthier and live the quality of life you hope for.

On the other side of the lake, you can see that there is a great deal of color, unlike the bleak side of the lake where you live. On your side of the lake, feelings are primarily unpleasant and unhappy, at least when you're by yourself and don't have to put on any masks. You've heard that life on the other side of the lake contains a full range of vibrant emotions. There is sadness, frustration and irritation, of course, but there is much joy, a lot of laughter, and a positive, hopeful outlook. People are active and busy, engaging in all kinds of activities they enjoy and are capable of doing. You long to live on that side of the lake.

29

In order to live there, you have to go THROUGH the lake. There's no easier, softer way. Going around the lake isn't possible (don't ask me why…I'm just making this up and those are my made-up rules)! If you want to have the kind of life you say you want (such as, oh…I don't know – living at a healthy weight and engaging in the sorts of activities you would enjoy)…then you have to go through the lake.

Did I forget to tell you what the lake is made of? DOO-DOO. It's a lake full of DOO-DOO and you have to go in until the DOO-DOO is up over your head before you can start walking out the other side to that life you want. So how bad do you want it?

What's the DOO-DOO? It's all the negative self-talk you engage in, it's the unpleasant memories from your entire life to this point, it's any criticism you endured, names you were called, times you were made fun of. It's any unpleasant thoughts, feelings, body sensations, and memories you have ever experienced. You have to go INTO them, (talk about them, cry about them, say good-bye to them, let them know they can no longer have power over you)…and then start walking out toward the experience of genuinely joyful living (which does include pain, but provides you with ways to deal with it in healthy ways). As you walk out the other side, the water is crystal clear and you wash away the DOO-DOO...

How badly do you want that life? How hard are you willing to work to get it?

Cari said it when she talked about needing to change your relationship with food. *Obesity isn't really about food...*

30

You Want it HOW Bad?

How badly do YOU want to live in Recovery From Obesity? How badly to you want to live at a healthy weight and enjoy an improved quality of life, being able to engage in activities you enjoy? How badly do you want a life that is not food-obsessed? What are you willing to do to obtain that kind of life?

Below is a list of things you "gotta do" if you want what you say you want. Review the list and be honest with yourself...how willing are you to do what it takes? Here's the deal: if you do every single thing on this list every day, I can guarantee you the life you say you want...If you do half the things on the list every day, you've got about a 50% chance...It's up to you!

31

1. Make healthy food choices.
2. Maintain portion control.
3. Exercise.
4. Drink water.
5. Eat breakfast.
6. Plan your meals and follow your plan.
7. Keep a food diary.
8. Keep an exercise diary.
9. Get enough sleep.
10. Use a healthy support system.
11. Get individual and/or group therapy.

RECOVERY

> RECOVERY BEGINS WHEN YOU STOP BEING AFRAID YOU CAN'T LIVE WITHOUT IT AND REALIZE YOU CAN NO LONGER LIVE WITH IT.

— CARI DE LA CRUZ

Q

"I have lost 135 pounds, but my weight loss goal was to lose 150 pounds. I have been able to achieve all of the other goals I've set in my life. I feel like a failure. How do I get to that goal?"

33

THE POST-OP SAYS

Ahhh, spoken like a true "Perfectionist." Of course, it takes one to know one, though I consider myself to be a recovering perfectionist (something I haven't yet perfected, but I'm working it...) Anyway, I have this theory about success and how we define it in our lives. After all, what you are really asking in your question is how can you be as successful (perfect) at losing weight as you have always been at everything else?

About now, you're probably thinking, "I had surgery, and I can't eat as much a I used to, so why am I still consumed by my thoughts, feelings, behaviors and relationship with food? Here's your answer: Because surgery doesn't address any of that stuff...it simply makes it more possible for **you** to address it – and it sounds to me like it's time for **you** to address it!

Well, I think that we (as a society) are very quick to define "success" in the very strictest, most conservative of terms, yet our definition of "failure" is incredibly liberal. What I mean is, there is a teeny, tiny margin of error in how we qualify as successes ("You must be a Size 0") but incredibly high odds of failure ("If you wear anything bigger than a Size 0 you are fat.")

Let me elaborate a little with an analogy. Let's say you're playing a game of baseball. Whoever gets the most runs, wins. Sounds simple enough. But what if the only way to score is by hitting a homerun? In other words, even if you get on base with a bunt or a walk, and then advance around the bases, you won't earn a point by sliding into home plate. Seems a little "pointless" to me, I mean, why bother trying to hit the ball if you know only a homerun will count? And why bother running the bases if you know your run won't count? Hmmm...that sounds like an incredibly limited definition of winning (success) and an extraordinarily unlimited definition of losing (failure.) Basically, if you play the game this way, it's gonna be impossible to win and even harder to stay motivated.

So, how does this apply to your weight loss journey and how you define success and failure? To me, it sounds like you're playing the game I described above and if you lose anything OTHER THAN 150 pounds you lose the game. What that means is, if you lose 136, 137, 138, 139, 140...149 pounds – by your own definition – you're a failure – until you reach 150, and then you magically become a success...until you regain a pound...Oh dear! Being successful is stressful the way you talk about it, and it doesn't sound like much fun, either. You know what? I wouldn't want to play by your rules so I think it's time to redefine them.

First of all, I'd get rid of that number. Yuck. It's way too limiting. I mean, your weight can fluctuate five pounds in one day, so according to your rules, you could wake up a winner and go to bed a loser (a great way to increase your odds of a nightmare.) That's why you should make your goal something that is not tied to the scale or a number on your clothing. I don't know...something like increasing your speed on your next walk around the block, or completing your first 5K, or ziplining, or going back to school to get your college degree, or maintaining a healthy weight that makes you AND your doctor happy. Those all seem pretty reasonable to me, but feel free to come up with your own.

The bottom line is, you need to acknowledge your extraordinary success (135 pounds lost) and begin to set new goals that you can actually achieve. Change those definitions of success and failure. Make it possible to succeed and harder to fail. No, I'm not saying to lower the bar – I'm saying recognize that what you're calling failure might really be success.

35

The comment about losing an exceptional amount of weight but not making "goal" is one we hear a lot! These kinds of statements tend to be about perfectionism. Perfectionism includes both thoughts and behaviors. Perfectionism is about having exceptionally strict standards and unrealistic expectations...maybe of yourself, maybe of others, and maybe of both yourself and others.

Perfection (or the attempt at perfection, since actual perfectionism is an impossible pursuit as human beings) is an example of a coping mechanism—one that, like most of our unhealthy coping skills—serves a survival purpose in childhood but does not work in adult life. Some children attempt to be perfect little people. They may do so for fear of being treated badly. Maybe as a small child you saw a brother or sister being treated badly by your parents when they misbehaved, so you tried to be extra good. Maybe you saw one parent treat the other poorly and you didn't want to be called names or yelled at so you tried to have perfect behavior. Children may try to be perfect to avoid feeling the painful emotions associated with being treated poorly, by parents, by other adults, or by peers.

Kids may try to behave perfectly in an attempt to get much-needed praise and attention. Maybe there were so many kids in your family that it was hard to get attention so you thought if you behaved perfectly you would get noticed. Maybe you tried to be perfect at school so the teacher or coach would praise you. Maybe you had a talent for singing so you tried to be perfect in your performance skills so you would be recognized for something positive. "Going for the Gold" in every single situation cannot work in adult life (and didn't work as a child, either). The need to be perfect leads to exhaustion. Because perfection isn't possible. Several researchers have discussed a variety of overlapping categories of perfectionism. The following were discussed by Elliot and Meltsner (1991) and Burns (1989) – not that you probably care where this information came from, but because I can't take credit for these! You may recognize situations from your own life that fit one or more type of perfectionism noted:

Moralistic perfectionism can be described by the statement, *"I must not forgive myself if I have fallen short of any goal or personal standard."* Gee! This sounds familiar! I do believe our question was, "I have lost 135 pounds, but my weight loss goal was to lose 150 pounds. I have been able to achieve all of the other goals I've set in my life. I feel like a failure. How do I get to that goal?" If the personal goal was to lose 150 pounds and the reality is a loss of 135, the person who is a realist, with healthy self-esteem will say, "My initial goal was to lose 150 pounds. I seem to have settled in after losing 135 pounds. My health has improved tremendously, the quality of my life is dramatically improved, I feel so much better and am able to do so many things I couldn't before the surgery. As long as I continue to put forth effort into the Gotta Do Em's, I will be proud of, and grateful for the positive changes in my life with my 135 pound weight loss."

Performance perfectionism says, *"To be a worthwhile person I must be a great success at everything I do."* Again, the question related to losing 135 pounds versus 150 pounds is an example of performance perfection. Additionally, the author of our question notes that they "have been able to achieve all of the other goals I've set in my life." I might have to pull an American Idol judge comment on them and say, "Perhaps your other goals have been safe." The judges on Idol say that the contestants chose a "safe" song when it was one they could easily sing well. Perhaps the other goals this person set were fairly easily attainable for that person...? 135-pound weight loss is a tremendous accomplishment, whether or not our author ever gets to a 150-pound weight loss.

Emotional perfectionism occurs when a person thinks, *"I must always try to be happy. I must control my negative emotions and never feel anxious or depressed."* I've had many a WLS patients tell me they have worked very hard to remain in control of their feelings at all times, particularly when dealing with other people. Part of that is attempting to people please in an effort to be liked. Emotional perfectionism can also be an attempt of feeling "okay" about yourself by remaining "in control" of your emotions when internally you may feel out of control emotionally. To deny frustrations, feelings of anxiety or sadness is to not be human.

Oh yeah–so is attempting to be perfect!

Identity perfectionism: *"People will never accept me as a flawed and vulnerable human being."* How often have you said or thought, "As long as I am obese, many others will not accept me."? I also hear a lot of post-ops talk about their frustration when people "who never gave me the time of day," "all of a sudden" talk to me "because I've lost weight." Sometimes I wonder if people struggle to accept themselves as much as they believe that others won't accept them due to being obese. (I also wonder how much differently they are presenting themselves as they lose weight and how much that contributes to other people's "acceptance" of them.) Just a thought…!

Appearance perfectionism: *"I look ugly because I'm overweight (or have heavy thighs or a facial blemish)."* Let me just say that appearance perfection is a sickness in our society, regardless of a person's weight. We all struggle with accepting our body in some way(s). For this, I can only say that if we focus on the things we are able to do (particularly after WLS compared to what was possible prior to weight loss) and if we simply look at a picture of a person missing a limb or on crutches or in a wheelchair or without capabilities that we have, then we can choose to be grateful. I struggle with my thighs (my right one in particular–I have no idea why)…but when I get the "bitch and moans" about my thigh(s) or any other part of my body, I remind myself to be grateful I have that part to do whatever its job is to do. I hope you will do the same!

PERFECTIONISM: *Where is this kind of thinking/acting going to get you?*

John Bradshaw, a man whose wisdom I greatly admire, refers to the "Rule of Perfectionism." Dr. Bradshaw says that the Rule of Perfectionism means, *"'Always being right' in everything you do." He explains, "No rule leads to hopelessness more powerfully than this one. The perfectionistic ideal is shameless since it disallows mistakes. Shame as a healthy human feeling lets us know we are finite and incomplete. Shame lets us laugh at our mistakes. Shame tells us we are always in need of feedback and human community. Shame lets us know we are not God. Shame lets us know we are human. Following the perfectionism rule leads to hopelessness because to be perfectly human is to be imperfect. Perfectionism is inhuman."*

So there you have it! Have you lost a considerable amount of weight and have improved health and an improved quality of life as a result? Then you are a WLS success! Enjoy it! Appreciate it! Do the Gotta Do Em's so you can manage your weight–regardless of where your body settles!

HoMeWork™
by APOD

Make two lists. One list is called **"Goals/Number Successes"** and the other list is called **"Goals / Life Successes."**

Under **Goals/Number Successes**, write what your number goals were (goal weight, clothing size desired, etc.) and place a check if you were able to meet your number goals. In the **Goals/Life Successes** column, write down some of the things you wanted to do to live a fuller life as a result of losing weight (ride a bike, fly without a seatbelt extender) and place a check if you have been able to accomplish your life successes.

(Here's a hint for you: Often, people set number goals that set them up to feel like failures because they set the goals too low. Therefore they feel like "failures." Life goals usually leave people feeling successful because they are able to do things they have long wanted to be able to do. This results in feeling like a winner.]

40

Goals/Number Successes		Goals/Life Successes	
❑		❑	
❑		❑	
❑		❑	
❑		❑	
❑		❑	
❑		❑	

HONESTY

" WE ALL MAY HAVE OUR DAYS WHEN WE FEEL AWKWARD OR UNCOMFORTABLE IN OUR BODIES, BUT THE KEY TO DEVELOPING POSITIVE BODY IMAGE IS TO RECOGNIZE AND RESPECT OUR NATURAL SHAPE AND LEARN TO OVERPOWER THOSE NEGATIVE THOUGHTS AND FEELINGS WITH POSITIVE, AFFIRMING, AND ACCEPTING ONES. "

– NATIONAL EATING DISORDERS ASSOCIATION

Cari De La Cruz & Connie Stapleton, Ph.D.

Q

"I lost 140 pounds after having RNY five years ago. I kept it off for three years and then I lost my job so the stress got to me and I gained back 50 pounds. Then I couldn't afford to go the gym so I couldn't work out any more and gained back another 30 pounds.

What am I supposed to do?"

Weight management would be easy if it weren't for a certain 4-letter word that we all know and use every day: L-I-F-E. It's true, I mean, we can't control what happens to us (even though we think we can or think we do), and that calls to mind another 4-letter word (which I won't use here because my mom will probably read this book). Wow, what a downer...well, stick with me because I'm not saying that we have absolutely no control in this life! I'm saying that, while we can't control what happens, we can control (or influence) what *we do about it.* In other words, while you don't have control over losing your job or not having enough money to go to the gym, you **do** have control over whether or not you eat more in response to this bad news.

Let's take "food" and "exercise" out of the equation and substitute something else for those responses to L-I-F-E.

What would happen if, every time you got a piece of bad news, you hit your big toe with a hammer, and every time you felt stressed out you kicked the dog (with the other foot, naturally)? I'm guessing your toe would hurt and the dog would bite you – negative consequences for your responses, right? Now, I know, you're saying, "But, I wouldn't smash my toe with a hammer, and I don't even HAVE a dog...and besides, those aren't reasonable responses..." Well, if kicking the dog was your "go-to" response, then trust me, you'd find a dog, and it would make perfect sense to you. And, if you saw OTHER people whacking THEIR toes with hammers, even though it might seem destructive and harmful, I'm betting that – even if you DID think it was stupid, you'd still do it. How can I say that? Well, a lot of people think overeating is stupid (but we do it anyway), and a lot of people think kicking dogs is a really bad idea (but...some of us do it anyway – not me). So maybe there isn't really a connection between the "LOGIC" or "REASON" behind the behavior and the actual behavior! In other words, the two things are not inexorably connected, so you can change the response!

What do you change it to? Let's start by making a list of practical, healthy, enjoyable behaviors. Ready?

My Next-Time-I'm-Stressed List

1. ~~Hold my breath until I pass out.~~ Okay, I don't like that one…I'm starting over.

My Next-Time-I'm-Stressed List (Do-Over)

1. Go for a walk around the block. I can stomp and clench my fists if I want to. I can even pump my arms and stride faster. Fun fact: Did you know that your feet keep up with your arms? So, if you swing your arms faster, you'll walk faster. True!

2. Iron something (like curtains or a tablecloth). Why not? I've been putting it off for a year!

3. Cry. Yes, this is valid and can be quite therapeutic.

4. Phone a Friend. They do it on game shows, why not do it in life?

5. Watch your favorite funny movie. I love When Harry Met Sally, So I Married an Axe Murderer, As Good As it Gets, Big, Ferris Bueller's Day Off, Music & Lyrics, What About Bob?

6. Watch your favorite sad movie. I refer you to number 3. But, here are some of my favorite sad flicks: Steel Magnolias, Terms of Endearment, Tristan & Isolde, Meet Joe Black, Braveheart, Saving Private Ryan. A good cry is worth a box of Kleenex.

7. Do something that's been on your wife's "Honey-Do" list for awhile. She's been asking you to vacuum behind the refrigerator and stove for sometime now…

8. Ride your bike. I love this one because you keep moving even when you stop pedaling. Catching a good wind in your face is a great way of blowing off "stink."

9. Sew that button back on your wool coat. You left it in your pocket last winter, remember?

10. Look at your before pictures. You did keep one, didn't you?

That's a reasonable list, but if you don't like it, write your own – now, before you need it.

So, there's your **Stress List**. Good, right? And those things don't cost money, so if you said you couldn't go to the gym because you didn't have money, there are plenty of "action items" you can do for free.

The point behind the list is, there is a ton of healthy things you can do to cope with stress, and they don't involve eating or flashing your gym card to Mr. 6-pack at the front desk. It's a matter of reframing your thinking. We obese (and recovering obese) people are conditioned to respond (react) in unhealthy ways when we feel out of control, yet eating junk food or skipping the gym doesn't give us the control we crave. That means it's time to make some new "connections" (you know, "When This happens, I usually do That."). Here's the goal: Pair 1 *Healthy Something* with whatever *Unhealthy Something* you encounter.

I'll give you a list of "L-I-F-E" Stuff (you know, things that happen and "make you" eat junk or avoid exercise) and then I'll show you "typical" responses (OLD) and "healthy" responses (NEW).

L-I-F-E Happens	OLD Unproductive/Unhealthy Destructive / Unhappy	NEW Productive/Healthy Productive/Happy
You forgot to pay the registration on your car and now there is a $150 penalty that you can't afford. (No, that didn't happen to me. Ever.)	Eat a bag of Oreos	Call an old friend (or a new friend).
Your car was making a horrible clunking noise and it finally died on the way home. Oh, and your AAA card gave you 7 miles, but you were 9-1/2 miles from the mechanic.	Go home and melt into the couch with a big bowl of popcorn.	Take a bike ride around the park.
Your boss called you into the office and chewed you out for something you didn't do	Go into your office, close the door, open a package of mini donuts and start complaining about your sucky life on Facebook.	Take a breather. Leave the office and either walk or drive to a quiet place to blow off some stink. Bring a protein shake or bottle of water for hydration.

L-I-F-E Happens	OLD Unproductive/Unhealthy Destructive / Unhappy	NEW Productive/Healthy Productive/Happy
You or your spouse lost their job.	This is scary. You're definitely going to want that ice cream. With walnuts and whipped cream. Better yet, make it Gelato.	This IS scary, but gaining 5 pounds over it is scarier. It's time to start learning how to meditate. C'mon, you know you've been threatening to do it for 2 years.
Your precious child just broke your favorite cut-glass vase and you cut your big toe on it.	Of course you're not going to hit that same toe with a hammer – it already hurts! Hit the other toe so you'll have matching pain.	Go get a pedicure. It's much happier for your toes.

You get the idea.

The point is, we can't expect healthy choices/thoughts and behaviors to just "happen." We need to do something to make the change, and that involves planning and preparation. Hey, when life HAPPENS, it doesn't always give us fair warning, and you know what they say, "The best offense is a good defense." Or, is it, "The best defense is a good offense"? Or, "Feed a fever, starve a cold…" Oh gosh, I always get those backward. Fool me once, shame on me. I'll leave it at that.

Here's the bottom line: You have more control (influence) than you think, so use it for your health and wellness and you'll be surprised how much better you feel about 4-letter words.

THE DOC SAYS

Well, all I can say is that Cari's 4-letter words are much nicer than mine! But, since her mom is going to be reading our book, I'll contain the use of my 4-letter words to fairly tame ones! I'm glad Cari focused on the word L-I-F-E. The author of this question has had some very unfortunate L-I-F-E circumstances. No doubt about that. And for that, I feel tremendous sadness, as losing a job is often a devastating situation. A person's response to unpleasant circumstances can fall into quite a wide variety of options. Some healthy...some less so. In this situation, unfortunately, the choice to use food to cope falls into the not-so-healthy category. This is an example of how having WLS without addressing underlying issues (in this case, eating when stressed), isn't always enough to help a person in the long haul! Had our author learned some healthy coping skills (such as those Cari proposed in her table...in the "NEW" column, in case you were wondering), then perhaps food would not have been the "go-to" when dealing with the loss of the job.

48

Cari covered the issue of learning healthier options when dealing with L-I-F-E, so I shall move on to another 4-letter word to be addressed in this situation. C-R-A-P! As in: It's crap to use life stress as an excuse for gaining 50+30=80 pounds. I realize that people turn to all sorts of unhealthy things in the name of dealing with stress. I did it for years, as well. So I'm not being judgmental–I'm just calling us all on it! We have other–healthier–options...if we seek them out, learn about them, and get help to use them.

The reality in this situation is not that stress caused the author to regain weight. The reality is that the author is not taking responsibility – is not being accountable–for their own behavior. This is what my job as the Doc is about...going a level or two deeper than the surface response, or the "common sense" answers. In this case, the surface response is, "I ate because I was stressed. My stress was related to a negative life situation." This makes it sound like the stress "made" the person eat.

So let's go deeper. The issues here appear to be:
1) taking responsibility (being accountable for) one's own behavior,
2) addressing whatever it is that prevents the person from taking responsibility,

3) *the feelings associated with losing the job, and*

4) *not getting help to deal with a difficult situation but instead choosing to cause self-harm (weight regain).*

I'll address the first and second issues I listed together. What makes people use excuses for their behavior? We do it all the time. Here is an example of making excuses: "You made me mad so I called you names." Here's the reality–without blaming you or making excuses for my bad behavior: "I called you names. Yes, I was angry with you but that does not force me to call you names. I chose to call you names even though I had many other options to choose from to handle my anger."

Here are other examples of making excuses for (not taking responsibility for) your own behavior: "I stopped going to the gym because you wouldn't go with me anymore." "If the kids didn't want junk food in the house, I wouldn't have to have it there." "If I had more time, I wouldn't have to go through the drive-thru so often to eat." See what I mean? And in the original example, the surface response (which is also what I'm referring to as not taking responsibility for one's own behavior) was: "I ate because I was stressed." The deeper, more honest and personally accountable response would be: "I used food to deal with stress because I don't want to (or know how to) deal with my feelings in healthy ways."

C-R-A-P.

We make excuses and blame other people because we don't want to take responsibility for our own poor choices. Why not? Because taking responsibility makes us accountable and who wants to own behaviors they're not proud of? Certainly not a person who already may feel badly about him or herself. If I already have a lot of shame about who I am (remember what I wrote about self-esteem earlier in the book?), then I don't want to reinforce to myself how poorly I feel about myself. Accepting responsibility for my own behavior only highlights how "bad," "awful," "wrong," "unworthy," and "despicable" I am. So I have to blame someone else, or outside circumstances, for my behavior.

How can this be corrected? It takes a lot of time, a lot of self-reflection (and/or therapy), and a willingness to ACCEPT yourself, flaws and all. And to realize that flaws do not make us "bad, unworthy, unlovable, or

49

despicable." A person with healthier self-esteem owns their behaviors: "I reacted poorly to that situation by losing my temper. I called you inappropriate names and I blamed you for my bad mood. I'm sorry I did that and am upset that I allowed myself to react that way. It would have been more appropriate for me to ask for a few minutes to calm myself down before we talked. I will work harder in the future to do that so this doesn't happen again."

In the case of the person who authored the question for this section, taking ownership of the behavior would (again) sound something like, "After losing a lot of weight following WLS, I returned to the unhealthy behavior of eating in response to stress. That resulted in my gaining 50 pounds. It would have been healthier for me to talk about the sadness, anger and embarrassment of losing my job instead of eating to try to ignore my feelings. Then I used the job loss as an excuse to quit exercising. It's true that I could no longer afford the gym, but there are plenty of free exercise options. The consequence of making excuses and continuing to use food to avoid my feelings was an additional 30 pound weight gain."

Now let's deal with numbers 3 and 4 from my list of "deeper issues" related to this person's situation:

3) *the feelings associated with losing the job, and*
4) *not getting help to deal with a difficult situation but instead choosing to cause self-harm (weight regain).*

Sometimes truly difficult situations happen. If the person who lost the job would have given themselves permission to talk about their feelings related to losing their job, perhaps they wouldn't have turned to food. However, as mentioned earlier, if a person already feels badly about himself then they are going to struggle to get R-E-A-L about their feelings. It's tough when a person already thinks they are "a loser," or "always unlucky," or "undeserving of good things" to avoid beating himself up over a job loss—even if the job loss was part of a company-wide downsizing or other situation unrelated to the person's performance. If the job loss was actually related to poor performance, it will be exceptionally hard to take responsibility for losing the job if one already has low self-esteem.

Regardless of the level of a person's self-esteem or the reason for losing the job, the loss of a position is difficult and everyone will have some feelings about it. If you don't talk about those feelings, then you will act out the feelings. If, as Cari noted, your "go-to" behavior is eating, then you'll likely turn to that. And the consequences will be what they have always been – weight regain.

Very often we are not equipped to handle difficult situations by ourselves. Especially if our past behaviors typically led us down the same unhealthy roads when we were hit with a tough predicament. As usual, that low self-esteem comes into play. If we're already "down on ourselves," as they say, then it's easy to do what we have done in the past when something negative happens: punish ourselves. If we've used food to punish ourselves in the past (which many people do), it's likely that we will again turn to food when present life circumstances get tough.

And then there's the fact that most of us were not shown by example healthy ways to deal with the more unpleasant and difficult times in life. Many of us saw adults drink to excess when the going got tough. Others saw adults hide in bags of potato chips, drown their sorrows in vodka or milkshakes, or overspend money, gamble or hoard in response to difficulties.

So it's up to each of us as adults to do as I always say: Get Help and Get Happy (or at least happier)! Take the responsibility to ask for help so you can 1) take personal responsibility for your own behavior, 2) address those things (low self-esteem, pride, etc.) that prevent you from taking responsibility, 3) address the feelings associated with life circumstances, and 4) get help to deal with those difficult situations in healthy ways.

If you're not able to simply apply one of the suggestions Cari gave, then get into therapy and work on the above issues while getting help to incorporate her healthy options!

P.S. You don't have to work through all of your issues before you can engage in choosing healthy behaviors...work on your issues and choose healthy behaviors at the same time.

Complete the questions:

1. If you are not exercising on a regular basis, state your reason(s):

   a. _____

   b. _____

   c._____

2. Now, go deeper than your "surface" responses and provide deeper, more honest and personally accountable responses:

   a. _____

   b. _____

   c._____

3. Are you courageous enough to answer these questions whenever you hear yourself "making excuses?"

   ❏ Yes, I am.

   ❏ No, I'm not.

HONESTY

" IN LOSING WEIGHT AND SUSTAINING THAT WEIGHT LOSS, YOU MUST BE DIRECT AND HONEST WITH YOURSELF, DO NOT PERMIT EXCUSES. "

– CONNIE STAPLETON, PH.D.

Q

"I struggle with 'head hunger,' and I know the difference between 'head hunger' and when my stomach is physically hungry. Bottom line to me is that I'm still hungry either way!"

The funny thing about head hunger is, even when I apparently have it, I still feel hungry. It doesn't feel any different from stomach hunger (I don't think), but I'm not sure. All I do know is: **I AM HUNGRY.** So, when I hear someone say that there is a difference between head and stomach hunger, I wonder if my stomach understands this difference, and if I am supposed to feel different when my head is hungry. Perhaps the problem stems from the fact that I never really learned what it means to actually be hungry; I just learned to eat. If you're anything like me, then you probably followed a similar protocol:

- It's lunchtime (eat).

- It's dinnertime (eat).

- It's dessert time (eat).

- It's Thanksgiving (eat).

- It's bedtime (eat).

- It's Monday (eat).

- It looks good (eat).

- It's raining (eat).

Uh-oh…I think I might be onto something here. Several of those feeding situations have nothing whatsoever to do with the level of fullness in my stomach, which means the problem isn't really the hunger at all; it's how I've been conditioned to understand hunger. I suspect you might be having the same problem and fortunately for you, this isn't the first time I've thought about this issue, so I have some ideas.

Now, from what I've gathered it all comes down to how we learned to respond to what we believe is hunger (which, I realize sounds dubious, but hear me out.)

Maybe it would be clearer if I put the information into a chart.

Symptom (Signal)	Interpretation	Solution
Grumbling Stomach	I need food.	Eat something substantial - like a sandwich!
Headache	I have low blood sugar.	Eat something with sugar - like a candy bar
Shaking	I need food.	Eat something fast. I obviously forgot to eat!
Sleepy Lack of Energy	I need food.	Eat something from the vending machine. I don't have energy to prepare something.
The Time	This is the time I always eat.	Eat!
Cranky/Bad Attitude	I must be hungry.	Eat something you love to improve your attitude...like cookies!
Bored	I'm probably hungry.	Eat!
Smell/Sight	I'm probably hungry.	That looks good! Eat it!
Price	I probably can't eat that much, but it sure is a good deal. I get more for less money!	Eat more!

57

Wow, I don't like that chart. It lies. I mean, who does that? Who eats when they aren't really hungry? Oh yeah, you and me. Since it appears that these habits are pretty well ingrained in most of us, our best hope for recovery is to recondition ourselves to respond differently to the familiar "hunger" signals. In order to do that, we're going to have to change the conversation, our thinking and our behaviors. Time for a little self-talk!

Wanna eavesdrop on my conversation with ME?

Conversation #1: *(Grumbly tummy)*

Me: My tummy is grumbling, I must be hungry.

Me 2: Wait a minute, that might not be true. When was the last time I ate something and was it healthy or junky?

Me: It was a long time ago…at least an hour…and it was a teeny, tiny handful of pretzels. Mini-pretzels, even.

Me 2: Uh-huh. That makes sense. So, did you eat those for your mid-morning snack, or something else?

Me: I'm not sure. They were there, so I ate them. But I would have eaten way more before, so I did good.

Me 2: Any protein in there…like hummus or something?

Me: Not really. I didn't want to eat too much.

Me 2: Well, I'm not surprised you're hungry because you didn't eat anything to sustain you. You had cheap carbs that burn up and burn out in a hurry. Is now a reasonable time for a meal, or would it be best to have a glass of water and wait until lunch?

Me: I guess I can wait…

Me 2: SUCCESS!

Conversation #2: *(Headache)*

Me: My head hurts. I think my blood sugar is low. I need to eat a Reese's Peanut Butter Cup.

Me 2: Are you hypoglycemic or diabetic?

Me: No. I'm just hungry. Whenever I get a headache, I know it's my blood sugar, so I have to eat candy.

Me 2: Actually, it might just be a headache. When was the last time you ate and what did you have?

[Are you noticing a trend here? I keep asking myself when and what I last ate.]

Me: I had Starbucks about 1½ hours ago, but there's protein in the milk!

Me 2:   Yeah, but you probably added whipped cream to it (which doesn't count as protein, because it has too much sugar in it). Was that your best choice? How about some cottage cheese and fruit?

Me: Okay...Peel me a grape.

Conversation #3: *(Price/Smell)*

Me: Oh my gosh! Those apple pies are on sale – 2-for-1! They smell so good! Man, I am hun-gry!

Me 2:   When was the last time you ate and what did you have?

Me :   This again? I drank a protein shake 2 hours ago, so it's time for me to eat.

Me 2:   Okay, but is it time to have apple pies?

Me: I'm only going to eat one now and I'll save the other one for later... or tomorrow.

Me 2:   How about some string cheese and some soy crisps?

Me: You really know how to suck the fun out of food.

59

Conversation #4: (Mad)

Me: I am SOOOOO mad at my boss!!! He is such a jerk. Oh, look! Somebody brought donuts! I'm hungry.

Me 2:   When was the last time you ate and what did you have?

Me: Do you even KNOW any other questions??? I don't remember, but I am CERTAIN I'm hungry.

Me 2:   Is it possible you are frustrated with your boss and only your head is hungry?

Me: Maybe, but it feels the same to me.

Me 2:   I don't think it does. Sit for 30 minutes and see how you feel about it then.

Me: 30 minutes is a long time, and the donuts might be gone by then.

Me 2:   True, so just wait.

In each of those conversations, I'm having a rational and calm discussion with myself–even if I don't feel calm and rational–because I've learned that logic sometimes helps diffuse a hunger crisis.

But, not always...

You and I both know there will be times when we absolutely know our heads are hungry and not our stomachs, but we'll eat something anyway. In those times, I suggest starting with water or a sugar free beverage (like Crystal Light.) See if that satisfies you. If it doesn't, then tell yourself you can choose something fun, but healthy...if you wait 30 minutes. This is not easy (obviously), but it IS doable.

So, how do you feel about talking to yourself?

Now, how do you feel about talking yourself out of that cupcake?

I'm glad we had this conversation.

THE DOC SAYS

❝Head hunger" and physiological hunger both indicate a "hunger" from within. When you are physiologically (or physically) hungry, your body is literally hungering for nutrition from food to provide nourishment for your body. Like a car needing gas, our bodies are designed to need fuel in order for us to keep running (or even just walking...and simply to keep living)! Sometimes people become a bit too much like the gas tank in a car. How? A gas tank has no idea whether or not it is full, ¾ full, ¾ empty, or "running on fumes." A gas tank doesn't feel anything. It just exists. Fortunately, we have a fuel tank indicator to let us know when we need to stop at the gas station and fill up. The gas tank itself doesn't care one way or another if it has too much or not enough gas. It just sits there, doing nothing, thinking nothing, and is completely out of touch with the fuel tank indicator you see on your dash board. We have to rely on this gauge to let us know when we'd better make time to stop and fill her up if we want to continue getting to where we need our vehicles to carry us.

Our brain is similar to the fuel gauge in a vehicle. The brain is what lets us know when our stomach is full or empty. Our brain gets signals from the stomach that says whether we are hungry, satisfied, or full. Sometimes, for a variety of reasons, our stomach becomes more like an inanimate, non-feeling feature of our body–like a gas tank. It doesn't know if it's full, empty, or somewhere in between. It quits interacting with the brain and just sits there, letting us put too much or too little food in it. And something goes awry with the fuel indicator (the brain). It can no longer tell when the stomach is empty or full. So we may go too long without eating. At other times we eat and eat, even though there is already plenty of gas in the tank.

When the signals get all mixed up in our bodies, and you don't know if your stomach is actually hungry or not, but you feel hungry frequently (even if you've eaten), you are probably experiencing "head hunger."

"Head hunger," means our bodies have sufficient fuel in the tank (you've eaten enough to keep your body running smoothly), but you believe you are still hungering for additional food. With "head hunger," it's likely that you are hungering for something, but it's probably not food. Nor will food fix the problem.

If the gas gauge on your car stops working, you're eventually going to run into trouble—most likely in the form of finding yourself stranded in traffic or on the side of the road because your fuel tank became empty and the car will no longer run—unless you take the car in to the service station and have the mechanic fix the gas gauge.

In the case of your stomach and your brain and the disconnect, the problems a person runs into vary. Some people quit eating and eventually don't take note of the signals from the stomach and/or ignore them or find ways to distract their brain. These people can become dangerously thin. For other people, even though their stomachs get plenty of food, they continue to eat and develop problems with being overweight or obese. In the scenario with a person and their body, the mechanic is a doctor. Actually—a team of doctors. One to check to make sure the body is properly functioning. If there are no medical reasons for the miscommunication between the stomach and the brain, another doctor is indicated: a therapist.

It's baffling to me, actually, that we all take our cars to mechanics because we know the consequences will be significant (and often costly) if we let the problem go but, when it comes to our bodies and our brains/emotions, we think things will somehow magically fix themselves. Look around at the number of people suffering from anorexia, bulimia, binge eating disorder, being overweight and obese—it's over 2/3 of our population! There is plenty of evidence that we ignore our bodies and our minds far too often. And the consequences are, indeed, costly.

Having said all that, let me now attempt to answer the question: Whether it's "head hunger" or physiological hunger, how does a person address these two issues following weight loss surgery (or when losing weight without surgery)? First, it's important that you follow your medical/surgical program's food plan following surgery. Once you are to the stage of eating solids, again, stick with what your doctors and nutritionists told you about eating. Some programs tell people to eat three meals and two or three snacks. Others say to eat five or six small meals every three to four hours. Either way is fine—as long as you eat healthy foods in the portions you were told to eat them. Always eat your protein first. Refrain from drinking with meals. If you "snack" at prescribed times, the "snack" has to be a healthy one, preferably containing protein! If you follow the eating plan your program recommends and eat healthy foods, there won't be a problem with biological hunger. Even if you do experience some degree of physical hunger, if you are following the program, you will have enough fuel for your body. Remind yourself that hunger is not an emergency, so long as you are following your healthy eating program and maintaining regular appointments with your physician, as well as taking the supplements your physician instructed. Tell yourself, "I will be eating again at __ o'clock and will be fine without additional food until then." It may help to set your watch to remind you when the next meal or snack is scheduled for. That way, there's no reason to continue thinking about food until the alarm goes off. After you've eaten, again set the alarm for the next scheduled eating time. This is just as important for the people who often skip meals or "forget" to eat as for those who tend to graze.

As for the "head hunger," if you are eating at the prescribed times and yet you continue to "think" you're hungry, there are other questions you can ask yourself to figure out what your brain is misconstruing as physical hunger. The best one may be, "What, besides food, am I hungering for?" Are you bored? Are you hungering for excitement or entertainment? Are you sad? Are you hungering for comfort? A kind word? A smile? A conversation? Are you scared? Are you hungering for reassurance? Do you need a hug? A friendly reminder that you are cared about? Are you stressed? Are you hungering for solitude? Do you need a short walk outside to clear you mind? Do you need a moment to say a silent prayer, to read a calming meditation or to repeat some positive affirmations? Learning what, besides food, you are hungering for, will lead you to an understanding of what, besides food, you may be wanting, needing, or craving. The next step is to learn to get your emotional needs met in healthier ways. (This may mean talking to a counselor!)

Head Hunger Habit

1. List the times when you eat purely out of habit (for example, when watching television, reading a book, etc.).

2. Create a written contract with yourself (and have a witness–who will support you and help you–sign it when you sign it) stating that eating during those times is not an option and you will seek assistance from your witness if you are tempted to eat at those times.

3. Generalize your ability to refrain from "mindless eating" at your most vulnerable times to refraining from eating any time and any place when you are not physically hungry.

SELF-TALK

> IF YOU'RE PREPARING TO SUCCEED FOR LONG-TERM WEIGHT LOSS THEN YOU BETTER GET STARTED MONITORING AND IMPROVING YOUR SELF-TALK!

— CONNIE STAPLETON, PH.D.

Cari De La Cruz & Connie Stapleton, Ph.D.

Q

"*Wow! Since WLS it seems like everyone is asking about my weight loss…people at the office, people at church, and of course, every member of the family. And when I go to my mother-in-law's house she gets upset if I don't eat the goodies she makes.*

Why is everyone so focused on me and my weight?"

Cari De La Cruz & Connie Stapleton, Ph.D.

THE POST-OP SAYS

In our world, how someone looks is a lot like religion; we worship celebrities because of their "perfect" noses, "perfect" abs, "perfect" legs, and "perfect" teeth. We believe the Victoria's Secret models actually LOOK like Victoria's Secret models, that people in the movies are taller than they appear in real life, and thin stars don't have to watch what they eat—or even work out. We sing the praises of the blessed ones who are miraculously endowed with perfection, and we tell our plastic surgeons we want to have St. Kim Kardashian's butt, Brother Matthew McConaughey's abs, and Sister Angelina Jolie's lips. We hunger for stories of those who have it all, but revel in the chance to sacrifice them when they "fall away from the faith," by exhibiting human frailties—like drug addiction, drinking and driving, and—heaven forbid—gaining too much weight, wearing a 2-piece bathing suit in public, or (worse) claiming that they actually "celebrate their curves."

68

Yes, in this society, "David" isn't made of marble or stone and works of art are no longer simply enshrined in a frame on a museum wall. Beauty is worshiped...on the computer, on television, in magazines, on Facebook, everywhere it can be displayed for all to behold. Ironically, this beauty we all crave is fleeting and temporary, age and weight gain are sins, and Photoshop is god, even though we desperately want to be young, thin and permanently Photoshopped ourselves.

When thin, attractive people are held up as gods, we mere mortals (especially obese ones) feel like the unwashed masses...peasants without any hope of salvation. Face it, not being what society says is heavenly can be a living hell.

And then one day, WLS saves us, and we begin to believe we'll have a chance to ascend the exalted throne for ourselves. We have faith that we will become perfect, slim, and carefree...like all of those royals (including the actual royals) in the magazines. We rejoice that we will finally see the light; we lose weight, we feel better, the choirs of angels sing, we're given a harp, undergo a supernatural transformation and then one day, even WE admit we don't recognize ourselves and have to pass a mirror twice, just to make sure it's us.

Why, then, do we get so upset when others NOTICE what we desperately wanted to see in ourselves? The truth is, we become curiosities–just like everyone else who dramatically changes before our very eyes. Aren't we entranced when people change their hair color? Awed when someone shaves his beard and moustache for the first time in 20 years? Dazzled when someone gets a new tattoo?

Think about it, don't you express wonder when you notice a radical change in someone else?

When we lose weight, we are elevated in the universe. For the earthbound, we become something of a spectacle…like a solar eclipse or shooting star. Like you, others begin to proclaim the good news–that something ordinary has become something extraordinary.

Now, imagine your child is obese. You spend 30+ years knowing them as they are then, seemingly overnight, they are no longer obese; they change. You don't recognize them. Holy cow! This is scary territory for a mom or dad, and they probably drop to their knees exclaiming, "Hallelujah! I'd always hoped for this, but never thought I'd see the day!" For 30+ years, they probably showered you with "food offerings,"–but now, you don't need those. They praised you with sacrifice–but you don't want those. Someone changed the dogma of the religion…And now, they are lost; they no longer understand the doctrine of your weight loss world. Now, combine that with the fact that many people around you suddenly feel like "sinners" because they are still obese and aren't living the gospel of good health! Hallelujah indeed! Pass the breadbasket…

What can you do about a society that worships all of the things you have become? Well, you DON'T preach to them. Instead, you inspire them so they understand the chapter and verse of your new life; you help them see the light of healthy eating, thinking and behaving. Soon enough, your transformation will stop being a novelty, your angel wings might get clipped, people (maybe even you) will stop taking endless photos of the new "god" (or "goddess") and life will return to normal.

If you're looking at WLS and weight loss as a curse, rather than a blessing, perhaps it's time to renew your own faith and remember why you chose it in the first place.

Cari De La Cruz & Connie Stapleton, Ph.D.

People certainly do get a lot of attention after WLS. The attention is often quite different than what they received before losing weight. Prior to weight loss, people get plenty of unwelcome negative feedback related to their weight. It seems strangers, family members and co-workers feel free to share rude comments, laugh at, and offer unsolicited advice to obese people. Equally painful, is the non-verbal attention obese people endure in the form of stares, pointing and disapproving looks.

It's no wonder many post-ops are uncomfortable with the attention they receive focused on their weight loss. After years of being the victim of negative feedback, they are now the recipients of positive, encouraging comments. There are countless questions about how such a remarkable feat of weight loss was achieved. Smiles, pats on the back, and thumbs up are showered upon the post-op as pounds melt away.

The comments, questions, and opinions of others can get to be a bit much for some people, particularly if they haven't had a lot of experience in setting healthy boundaries with people. And trust me—most people have not been taught, or shown how to set healthy boundaries with others. Yet learning to do so is beneficial in all areas of life.

Let me explain the concept of boundaries. Think about boundaries as a fence around a yard with a house in the center. The yard is your life. You are the house. The fence is there to let people in or to keep them out. You are the builder of the fence. If your fence has no gate for entry or exit, no one can enter or leave. If you put a fence with no gates around your life, you have built boundaries that are referred to as being "rigid." We usually have rigid boundaries when we don't feel safe or comfortable or want to control a situation. For example, when a person who is a yo-yo dieter is in a "fat phase" they tend to implement such boundaries. They stay home, spending as much time as possible there, interacting with as few people as possible. Often the goal is to prevent dealing with the negative feedback from others. It may be to avoid hearing a critical mother say, "If you continue to gain weight, you'll be looking like Aunt Rita in no time, and you'll be the one everyone's talking about." Hiding behind a rigid boundary (staying away from people as much as possible) may prevent being the victim of unwanted jeers, stares and embarrassing name-calling. While minimizing these sorts of negative interactions, isolating oneself is not a healthy way to live. We all need interaction with others; we need to give and share feedback, to talk and to listen, to encourage and to be encouraged. When we have a fence around our lives that has no entry, we have set boundaries that are too tight, or "rigid," and that keep people away from us and keep us isolated from other people. This is not a healthy way to live.

If we neglect to build a fence around our house and yard, then anyone is free to come and go as they choose. This is the case in the life of a person who allows others to take advantage of them. For example, this is the mother who always volunteers at the school and then often feels resentful that people expect so much of them. It's the teenager who offers to drive their group of friends everywhere but never asks for gas money. It's the guy who lends his truck to friends and neighbors but won't ask for help moving his old washer and dryer from the basement. This is the person who wants to be wanted, needed, liked or appreciated but doesn't know how to get those needs met appropriately. This is a person with no boundaries. This is any person who does not appropriately confront people who make unsolicited, rude comments to them, who allows others to offer unwanted advice, and who permits people taking physical or emotional advantage of them—all in an effort to feel liked, wanted, appreciated, or loved.

Some obese people fall into this category. Obese people can feel like others take advantage of them. They may not be setting healthy personal boundaries for themselves, fearing they will be alone, abandoned, not acknowledged, not included, and not liked. As a result, others do often take advantage of them. If this is to change they must learn to set boundaries.

When an obese person loses weight, they still have normal healthy emotional needs to be included, to be acknowledged, and to be liked. Their way of getting these needs met sometimes takes on a new look. The newly thin person can still be taken advantage of unless they learn to set healthy boundaries. Losing weight does not have the benefit of automatically instilling healthy behaviors!

A healthy person builds a fence around their house and yard but leaves a gate (or two) and puts locks on the gates. This allows for a person to have solitude when they want or need to ("shut people out"). It also allows a person to come and go, as well as to let people enter and leave. This is a person who is willing to say to their family member who criticizes their weight, "I appreciate your concern for me, yet I would prefer that you talk to me directly about your concerns rather than preach to me and compare me to deceased relatives." A person with healthy boundaries tells people, "When you expect me to drive to every basketball game, I feel taken advantage of. If I drive, I need everyone to chip in for the gas." A person with healthy boundaries says, "I appreciate your enthusiasm for my weight loss but would ask you not to comment on it when the break room is full of other employees." Building a fence with gates is a healthy balance between having no boundaries and having rigid boundaries. The healthiest place to be in life, most of the time, is in the middle.

72

If the attention you are receiving as you lose weight following WLS is uncomfortable for you, then get help in learning to set healthy boundaries. You may need to learn to deal with feedback in many different forms. Learning to set healthy boundaries is a skill that will benefit you in every single relationship you have in your life. This is a benefit to you in every area of your life! And certainly in every relationship! There are some great books on learning to set healthy boundaries. And the HoMEWork that follows will give you a good start in learning to set healthy boundaries.

Creating Healthy Boundaries

Write a boundary statement for each of the following situations:

1. Example: Your grandmother "insists" that you eat her special dessert.

   a. Your boundary statement: *"I hate to hurt your feelings, grandma, by not eating this delicious dessert. I need to care for my health and right now I can't eat anything with sugar in it."*

2. Your spouse continues to bring you unhealthy, fattening "treats," even though you have asked them several times not to.

   a. Your boundary statement: _____

   _____

3. The people at your office continue to ask, "How much more weight do you plan on losing?"

   a. Your boundary statement: _____

   _____

4. Your support group friends are giving you a difficult time when you opt out of a social engagement because your children have expressed a desire to spend more time with you.

   a. Your boundary statement: _____

   _____

5. Your preacher's secretary continues to ask you to head up a committee, even though you have respectfully declined several times.

   a. Your boundary statement: _____

   _____

73

Cari De La Cruz & Connie Stapleton, Ph.D.

HARD WORK

" DO NOT CONFUSE THE WAY I LOST WEIGHT WITH THE WAY I KEEP IT OFF. I LOST WEIGHT WITH THE AID OF WLS AND HARD WORK. I KEEP IT OFF THE SAME WAY EVERYONE ELSE DOES: **HARD WORK.** "

– CARI DE LA CRUZ

Q

"Sometimes it seems I've eaten something before I've even thought about whether or not I even want it! I have tried to stop doing this, but since I don't even know when I'm doing it in the first place, I'm really having a hard time.

Does anyone else struggle with this?"

75

THE POST-OP SAYS

I was driving home from work the other day (a route I've taken for 16 years) and noticed something I'd never seen before. It wasn't anything earthshattering, just a massive, 10 story building with a neon sign blinking on the top floor–but I was convinced it had magically appeared...that day. But, as if that weren't bad enough, for one scary moment, I became disoriented, didn't recognize where I was, and thought I'd gotten lost! Can you imagine that? Me and about a million other cars in bumper-to-bumper traffic...five miles from home and I was certain I'd never been there before.

Has this ever happened to you? Have you ever noticed something that has probably always been there, but you never saw it before that particular moment? Well, if you haven't, you're probably under 30, but if you have, then you'll understand how easy it is to forget where you put your reading glasses, why you walked into the room, what you were looking for in that cupboard, why you didn't pay the gas bill this month...and how you ate that entire bag of chips without even noticing. Heck, you can't remember chewing OR tasting, but your fingers are definitely orange, there is incriminating "gold dust" on your jeans, AND you have no idea what the "best by" date is!

Note: As I write this, I'm eating peapods from the bag and I've lost count. I think I'll eat just one more, then seal them up and put them back on the shelf.

Now, where was I? Oh yes, I was talking about how easy it is to forget stuff (like food you just ate), which means the answer to your question, "Do other people experience these things?" must be: "NO."

Okay, I'm kidding. If I remember correctly, the actual answer is, "YES. Sadly...YES." So, what's the solution? Well, I have a couple of thoughts (one of which I obviously didn't do above!)

Suggestions to Avoid Mindless Eating (because that's what it is):

1) Don't eat directly from the bag or package. Measure your serving and store the rest.
2) Plan what you'll eat before you eat it, otherwise, you'll be wide open to "That-Looks-Good-Syndrome" (which is what happens when you eat something "just because it looks good.")

3) Talk to yourself–out loud. "I am going to have a portion and will put the rest away."

4) Chew slowly and taste what you eat. If you're like me, you probably grew up thinking your stomach had teeth, so you could swallow everything whole and worry about digestion later. This is not true, so I suggest chewing well. It just tastes better that way…

5) Comment on the taste after each bite. Okay, this could get annoying around others, so maybe just comment in your head. "These peapods are crunchy and lightly salted. They taste good with my cottage cheese. I want to remember how good they are, so I will think while I eat."

I stopped at five because it's an even number. That, and the fact that number five sounded a little silly and number six wasn't sounding any better. but, hey–it's half my book, so I wrote my own rules.

It's the Doc intervening here…apparently it's not just me who has trouble with numbers…but I did check this one with my daughter–a college math major (takes after her daddy)–and she told me that five is definitely an odd, not an even number!

*Post-Op Here: I meant **round** number, not **even** number. It sure is a good thing I'm the one formatting the book so I get the last word.*

Back to mindless eating. How the heck does it happen in the first place? The short answer is, "Auto-pilot." Just like driving home from work, we flip the auto-pilot switch "on" (and sometimes even set cruise-control) and, like magic, we arrive at our driveway before we know it–which might explain why, in California, there is a law against holding your cell phone and talking while you are behind the wheel. Guess what? There is probably a little logic there because we often do the same thing with food while we are in front of the television or at the movies, or the plate. Unless you are a woman (sorry, guys), chances are, you can't focus on two things at once, so you probably choose to pay attention to what's on the screen instead of what's in your hand. Okay, I probably have to mention the remote control here, because men do have a preternatural ability to operate the remote while they are asleep on the couch, so...perhaps both sexes are equally adept at doing things without thinking.

And that can only mean one thing: **Don't eat unless you're thinking about it.** I hate those obvious answers because they seem so...obvious. But, like the Nike ads that tell you how to work out (Just Do It.) the only way to overcome mindless eating is to eat mindfully. You probably rolled your eyes when I said that (I did), but it's true, and it's a very grown-up thing to do. Like making healthy choices. Now, if you'll excuse me, there's also a law against texting while driving, so I'd better stop writing this before I get a ticket.

THE DOC SAYS

I love reading Cari's answers before I write mine because they always make me smile and put me in a fun state of mind before I type out my responses. Mind you–I am sitting (with very poor posture) on a bed with my feet under the covers and head phones in my ears so I can listen to beautiful Jim Brickman piano as I work. All that to say I am not texting my response in the car like certain not-to-be-named Post-Ops!

As much as some people want to throw up a little in their mouths (like certain Post-Ops) when they hear the word mindfulness, that is exactly the psychological tenet to be applied to this situation. It is one of those words that is everywhere in the psychological literature these days, and, like other words currently in vogue, tends to get overused. So let's make up an APOD saying for mindfulness...like paying attention! OK– that's what we'll do...whenever I'm tempted to type in mindfulness, I will instead talk about paying attention to what you're doing.

79

In addition to paying attention to what you're eating and when, we have to talk about breaking bad habits and forming new ones. So many of us have habits we are so used to that we're not even aware that we do them. For example, I tend to rub my feet together or simply move one of my feet back and forth when I'm sitting on the couch (yes, with my dirty feet right up there on the couch with me). It drives my daughter crazy and she's forever nagging at me to stop if she's on the couch with me. I'm not even aware I've been doing it! It's a habit of mine.

For lots and lots of WLS folks, eating without paying attention is a common (unhealthy) habit. Establishing a new habit or breaking a habit requires–yep–paying attention (see how much nicer that is than saying being mindful)!

Let's talk for a minute about why bad habits are hard to break and establishing healthy new habits are just as hard to implement. Well, let's start with the old *Dictionary.com* definition of habit, which is "an acquired behavior pattern regularly followed until it has become almost involuntary." I'm going to focus on the word "acquired." Think first about where you acquired your habits. Did your parents have some of the same "habits" that you do? How about the people you spend the most time with? (Like my proclivity to use 4-letter words…I come from a family of potty mouths!) Have you started using some of the same language that the people you hang out with use? (Look at Cari and her recent acquisition and use of colorful 4-letter words!) Some of our habits are learned behaviors. Some of them we figured the whole world had because we saw them from the day we were born. (Holiday traditions are an example of habits…we tend to bring our holiday tradition habits into the families we create as adults much like we do some daily habits.)

It's also important to be sure you are ready to change. If you're not really ready, but you embark on a change (like quitting smoking, beginning an exercise program, or yes–having WLS to lose weight), then you are going to be extremely frustrated and may not follow through with the behaviors necessary to obtain your goal. This will likely decrease future successes because if you "fail," then you may doubt your ability to ever follow through. (And this happens all the time with WLS patients.) There's a lot more to be said on this point alone, but alas–this book requires short answers so you'll have to wait and read more about that in a future book!

So–to break the habit of eating without paying attention (yeah–that thing referred to as mindless eating) check in with yourself and ask yourself, "How motivated am I to break this habit?" Do the same with any habit you are breaking or new behavior you are working to make part of your routine. Ask yourself, "How motivated am I to _____?"

Look at where you are in your life. Are there some seriously stressful events that may make this more of a difficult time to break a bad habit or implement a new one? Not that stress is an excuse for poor choices!!!! However, if you are going to try to stop smoking and your parent is critically ill, perhaps you might want to put off the smoking cessation until there is a change in that situation. In terms of your unhealthy eating habits, if you've already had WLS, then you need to make the effort to pay attention to what and when you eat no matter what is happening in your world!

Another important issue before you break or implement a behavior is to check your expectations. Are your expectations realistic? For example, is it realistic to think you will never eat a bite of food that is nutritionally empty ever again in your life? If you said that you do expect to never eat another bite of nutritionally empty food ever again, I'd say that would be an unrealistic goal. A more realistic goal would be to carefully choose limited occasions when you will opt to have a small serving of non-nutritious foods.

I've said it before and I'll say it many more times: Awareness is the first step of change. So start paying attention to what you're eating and when you're eating it! If you aren't hungry or have selected something that is unhealthy (given your goals of improved health and an improved quality of life), then get rid of it! Awareness followed by a wise decision based on moving in the direction of your values...that's what we're working toward here!

In This (Very) Moment

For one day, set your alarm for every hour that you're awake. When the alarm goes off, no matter what you are doing at the time, start being mindful (paying attention) and ask yourself these questions:

1. How do I feel right at this moment (emotions: mad, sad, happy, scared, discouraged, enthusiastic, etc.)?

2. What are my physical sensations ("pit in my stomach," heart beating rapidly, serene throughout, etc.)?

3. What am I aware of in my surroundings (sights, sounds, smells, touch, tastes)?

82

When you are engaged in various tasks (not just for one day–every day)–pay attention to your thoughts, feelings, and bodily sensations. This may sound silly, but you'll learn a lot about yourself. The more you become aware of what you are thinking, how you are feeling, and what your body is experiencing, the more you can monitor your responses and reactions to what's happening at the moment. And you will learn to live in the moment, which is all we have. Most of us spend so much time focused on the past or the future that we let our real life–our present–slip past! So next time you take a shower, pay attention to the water on your skin. When you eat, savor the flavors and textures of the food. When you're finished eating, move on to whatever you're doing next, and give whatever is next (your current present moment) all of your attention.

VIRTUE

"IF YOU WANT TO BE A VIRTUOUS PERSON, YOU DO THE THINGS VIRTUOUS PEOPLE DO. IF YOU WANT TO BE AN EDUCATED PERSON, YOU DO THE THINGS EDUCATED PEOPLE DO. IF YOU WANT TO BE A HEALTHY PERSON WITH A HEALTHY WEIGHT, YOU DO THE THINGS A HEALTHY PERSON AT A HEALTHY WEIGHT DOES: EAT RIGHT AND EXERCISE."

– CONNIE STAPLETON, PH.D. (Eat It Up!)

83

Cari De La Cruz & Connie Stapleton, Ph.D.

Q

"Why is it so important to talk about my childhood? I'm doing great in my life, especially compared to the rest of my family. I'm trying to lose weight, not relive things that happened years and years ago."

85

Cari De La Cruz & Connie Stapleton, Ph.D.

THE POST-OP SAYS

don't know about you, but I am really craving a bowl of Froot Loops. You know, those brightly colored, sugar-coated, life-preserver-shaped, floating spoonfuls of goodness? What do you mean, you don't like them? How could anyone **NOT LIKE FROOT LOOPS?** How could anyone not love the way they turn the milk into a rainbow-grey swamp when they swell? How could anyone not love the way they make you feel after you eat them? Didn't everyone's mom buy the assortment of mini cereal boxes when the family went camping during the summer? Didn't your brother always steal the *Froot Loops, Frosted Flakes, Lucky Charms, Trix, Cap'n' Crunch* and *Cocoa Puffs*, and leave you with the *Cheerios, Raisin Bran, Grape Nuts, Corn Flakes* and *Shredded Wheat*?

What? This didn't happen to you? I'm stunned. I thought this was a right of passage, but clearly it sounds like a...wrong of passage.

Huh. I wonder if there is something "to" this...?

Ohhhhh, wait a minute...I have a feeling this is one of those "me-issues"... the sort of thing that only makes me get weak-in-the-knees. Am I the only one who hears those adorable little bobbing inner tubes of comfort call out when passing them on the cereal aisle in the store? Doesn't Toucan Sam know everyone on a first name basis?

I can see where this is going. The innocent little box of sugary cereal has nothing to do with the cereal, and everything to do with how I think about the cereal. Basically, this boils down to justice, fairness, compassion and value.

Seriously? Cereal? I think we have to dig a little deeper into that cereal box, because there HAS to be a toy at the bottom. But, in order to fully understand my affinity for Froot Loops, you're going to need a little background information. My big brother is 3 years and 10 months older than I am. During the summer, my mom and dad used to take us camping. I should really say my DAD used to take us camping and my mom came along, because she really wasn't much of the "outdoorsy-type." That's important to understand, because it explains why she always packed her light-up make-up mirror and why we had a port-a-potty in the tent. Oh, and my brother is a Type 1 diabetic, which explains the need for packing instant-sugary foods (like Froot Loops.) At least, that's what I thought.

So, travel with me...back to Big Sur State Park. We are in camp, sleeping in a 4-man tent. There we are, waking up on our first cold morning in camp. My dad has a fire smoking–uh, burning–and my mom is doing her makeup at the picnic table, and my brother is already eating a bowl of cereal. Not just ANY cereal...he is eating...FROOT LOOPS. But, that's okay, I will get my very own box of Froot Loops (so we can both have the exact same thing.) What? There's only ONE box of Froot Loops in the assortment? Well, I guess I'll have to have Lucky Charms instead. I love those little marshmallow shapes and the–what? There isn't a box of Lucky Charms either? What about...Nope. Every single box of FUN cereal is mysteriously missing. But, it's only the first day, and no one else is eating cereal but my brother.

So, where did the other 10 boxes of sugary goodness go?

I am very sad. My vacation is off to a very bad start because I do not have a box of fun cereal and my brother has the one I wanted. Worse, he has all of the ones I wanted and I am left with Special K.

Here is what my 5-year old self thinks about not getting the Froot Loops: *Why don't I get the special cereal? Aren't I special? Didn't mom buy some for me? Oh, my brother has a medical condition and he needs the sugar when he has a reaction. That makes sense. I just have to be glad I'm not diabetic, too, or else I'd have to take insulin and drink orange juice when my blood sugar drops.*

Conclusions:

- My brother got the special cereal because he is very sick. (COMPASSION)
- I shouldn't feel jealous of my brother getting the cereal because he needs it. (JUSTICE)
- I am not very sick, so I should feel lucky. (FAIRNESS)
- I didn't get the special cereal because I'm not ...special? (VALUE)

How **else** could a 5-year old interpret the dynamics of the situation?

I'm supposed to feel bad for my brother. I'm supposed to "understand" that he has special needs. I am not supposed to be jealous because he is my brother. I am supposed to believe that my parents know best. I am supposed to feel lucky that I am not sick.

As I write that analysis, I get a little sad, because I realize that is actually what I believed. But, I didn't STOP believing it when I got old enough to understand differently, because by that time, the beliefs were already engrained; I was well-trained. Now, before we go any further, it's important for you to know that my parents did not knowingly do anything wrong; they were focused on a very sick child and times were scary. In those days, I remember our whole world revolved around his needs and the fact that he could DIE at any moment if his blood sugar wasn't tracked properly, or he didn't eat right, or he didn't get his insulin injection on time. He came first because…he HAD to.

Well, that may have seemed true, but the reality is very different.

He was sick, and he had extremely challenging needs–but, did he NEED the Froot Loops? Maybe.

Did he need ALL of the special cereals? No.

Could my mom have divvied them up at the start of the trip? Yes. She could have said, "Okay, last time you picked first, so this time your brother picks first." She could have decided NOT to buy the sugar cereal because we never had it at home, so why did we need it now?

You know what I learned from my mom's innocent and LOVING little decision? I learned that vacation means you get to eat junk food that you don't normally get to eat at home. It also means that you'd better hoard it before someone else gets it first, and you should feel guilty for wanting to take it away from someone else who "needs it" more.

I'm am 100% certain that was not my mom's intent. And I am 100% certain my mom and dad didn't value me less, or expect me to have more compassion that anyone else. I am 100% certain that my brother didn't wish for me to be sick like him. And I am 100% certain my family did not want me to grow up with unhealthy attitudes about myself and food. But, as we all learn (especially when we become parents ourselves), what we WANT or DON'T WANT for our children really doesn't matter–if we are

88

unhealthy ourselves. We can't control what our kids think and feel, but we can shape their responses to the input. If my mom and dad had known the things I was thinking, I know they'd have done everything in their power to help me understand that their love for me was not contingent upon, marginalized by or penalized because of their love for my brother.

But 5-year olds don't think that. Neither do 40-year olds. Unless someone helps them to understand better. I needed someone to help me understand. I needed someone to show me that I had the tools to unearth the sources of my beliefs. I needed them to help me to see that just because I didn't get FROOT LOOPS when I was 5, didn't mean that I SHOULD have them anytime I wanted to now! I needed someone to point out that eating Froot Loops as an adult wouldn't make me feel better about myself, wouldn't make me more valuable to my family, wouldn't help me feel deeper compassion for others, and certainly wouldn't improve my health.

You know, it's funny, but deconstructing the emotion and thoughts behind the Froot Loops has really helped me examine OTHER "beliefs" in my life, and I've learned that many of the things I held as TRUTHS were nothing more than distorted conclusions of a 5-year old. It feels good to grow-up. You know what? I don't think I want those Froot Loops after all.

89

THE DOC SAYS

I love how Cari illustrates the main point with stories and analogies. It's so much more fun to read than the dry, psychological answer. But both perspectives are important, so here I go with the less entertaining, but equally important educational part of the answer. Thus is the benefit of A Post-Op & A Doc...as we always say, *"It's good to know and even better to understand!"*

In order to deepen your understanding of why it's so important to talk about your childhood, regardless of how well (you think) you're doing in your present life is because, as Cari pointed out, our present feelings, reactions, responses and behaviors very often have roots to other situations, people, places, events and feelings from our past.

That's the short answer. But it really sums it up. Think about it... I'm sure you've often watched somebody else "overreact" to something. We might wonder, "What is she making such a big deal out of?" We might listen to a friend who is quite upset about something and think, "I don't get it. What is all the fuss about?" Trust me—other people have thought the same about you—and about me—at times.

Let me give you some examples from patients I have worked with. Recently a husband and wife were arguing in my office. Mrs. Jones (not her real name) was upset because Mr. Jones (not his real name, either!) had a habit of asking her what time she would be home when she went out to dinner with her girlfriends. This infuriated Mrs. Jones. She wasn't just frustrated with the question (which some people might see as a reasonable reaction). She was livid any time he asked her what time she would be home—from almost anything. Her reaction was "over the top" given the simple nature of his question. (I promise he wasn't being controlling or overbearing... if he had been, I would have addressed that.) We talked about what it was about the question, "What time will you be home?" that upset her so greatly. It turned out that her father would ask her that same question long after she was old enough to make her own decisions about when she would be home (she was in her early 20's and already living on her own and her father would "keep tabs on me," as she said). Any time her husband would ask what time she was going to be home, even though he was merely wanting a ball-park estimate, she would become enraged. She never understood her intense reaction until we discussed it that day in my office.

Granted, she wasn't reacting to something from her childhood necessarily, but her reaction in the present, which was an over-reaction given the current circumstances, was triggering feelings from a prior time. Because she had not ever confronted her father about her frustration, and had never verbalized how upset she had been with him for micro-managing her whereabouts in her young adult life, she expressed her (unidentified) anger at her father onto her husband. Her husband's question triggered her emotions about her father's over-parenting her. By becoming aware of, and acknowledging her anger toward her father, she was able to understand that her husband was not attempting to control her as her father had and realized that giving him an idea of when she would be home is a reasonable expectation for married couples. She was then able to provide that information to him without an angry outburst.

Another patient, Margaret (no, this wasn't her real name) asked one of her best friends to be a support person in her weight loss program. Susan, the friend, accepted. The two women discussed the role Margaret envisioned for Susan and they agreed that if Susan did not hear from Margaret by 10 PM each evening, Susan was to call and ask Margaret what healthy decisions and what unhealthy decisions had she made that day. Even though Margaret had asked Susan to do this exact thing, she found herself in tears any time Susan called and asked. In therapy, Margaret confided that after she got finished crying, she would "cuss her out in my head." Margaret couldn't understand her reaction or her behavior. She wanted Susan to help her. She loved and trusted Susan and knew that Susan had only her best interests at heart.

After some digging into the issue, Margaret realized that her mother used to point out to her most nights the things Margaret could have done that day to work on her weight. This went on from the time Margaret was in middle school until she left home at the age of 17. Now, at 54 years of age, she made the connection between how she felt as a child and how she felt when Susan called her and asked about her eating and healthy choices for the day. "I used to go to my room every night after my mother gave her 'daily suggestions,' as she called them. I would cry and then bury my head in the pillow and call her bad names. That's practically the same thing I'm doing now after I talk to Susan!" We were able to help her talk about her sadness and anger toward her mother. Then we discussed how Susan was not Margaret's mother, but a loving friend from whom she wanted help. We talked about Margaret's healthy decision to get help from a friend and how wonderful it was she could openly admit to the healthy and unhealthy choices she made during the day. In addition, Margaret noticed that noting her behaviors out loud was helping her become more aware of her choices during the day and that she was, in fact, making more and more healthy choices. She enjoyed being able to share being proud of herself with her friend who was genuinely excited with, and for Margaret.

We are very often unaware of how past "issues," (experiences, feelings, thoughts) impact our present thoughts, feelings, and behaviors. But I promise you the past has a very strong influence on our present. (Read *Living the Truth* by Keith Ablow for a wonderful book that helps explain this topic.)

The next time you witness someone else seeming to "overreact" to something, you can pretty safely bet they are not only reacting to the present situation, but there is something from their past fueling their reaction.

The same is true for you. If you find yourself have a reaction out of proportion to the situation at hand, it would be a good idea to ask yourself questions such as, *"When have I felt this way in the past?", "Has anyone else ever said that same thing to me?",* or *"Whose voice am I really hearing–the person talking to me or someone from my past?"* When we are "over-reacting," it's because we are reacting to the combination of thoughts and feelings related to the present situation and the intensity of years worth of feelings related to some past situation.

That's why it's important to talk about your childhood–so you can quit responding (childishly?) to some present, adult situations. As Cari noted–it feels good to grow up!

– Bonus Answer –

The Doc–with yet another response to the same question…(because I answered a similar question, which we discarded for the book and I didn't want to waste my response)!

You know…I hear so many patients share stories in which parents say and do horrible things to children. I swear one of these days I am going to write a book (yes–another book) called *Parents–Pull Your Heads Out!* (And yes–I do mean pull your heads out of the place where the sun don't shine!)

Having said that…let me back up and be a little nicer. From a compassionate standpoint, I am aware that any parent who treats their child in an abusive way (and in case you're wondering, name-calling and belittling a child is abusive)–has to feel absolutely horrible about him or herself. I also know that if a parent feels horrible about him or herself, that's it is probable that their parents (and/or others in their lives) also hurt them in some profound way(s).

And sadly, such is life. We have wounded people who grow up; then, from their own woundedness, they emotionally and/or physically wound the next generation. And so it goes…and we see the woundedness expressed in alcoholism, drug addiction, workaholism, sex addiction, gambling addiction, hoarding, shopping addiction, and obesity. (Depressing, isn't it?)

UNTIL someone along the way GETS HELP AND GETS HAPPY! In this case, that someone is YOU! YOU are saying, "I'm tired of living as an obese person and I am willing to do whatever it takes to stop this–for myself and for my next generation. I am a PIONEER!"

I say, "THANK GOD FOR THE PIONEERS WHO ARE WILLING TO DO THE HARD WORK TO MAKE THE CHANGES NECESSARY FOR IMPROVED OVERALL HEALTH."

93

Ah–I have digressed. For anyone who has repeatedly been told they won't amount to anything, it's darned hard to change that long-standing internalized belief. This just means that you've heard it ("you'll never amount to anything") over and over, probably in a lot of different ways– AND that you have come to believe it (you have internalized a message that came from an external source).

So again–the way to get past that message is two-fold. First, you have to realize that you were not born with the internal belief that you would never amount to anything (remember the Cup). The message that you'd never amount to anything came from someone important to you and may have been reinforced by other people (for example, a coach saying you aren't meant for baseball or a teacher saying you're not college material). We were all born to believe we are worthwhile–not because of what we can DO but because we are a human being. So–like with weight regain– it's back to the basics! In this case, the basic message is that you need to remember that you were born with the ability to believe in yourself. Now you have to make a conscious decision to remind yourself of that.

Next, you will need to remind yourself any time you find yourself thinking or saying something negative about yourself that the negative messages originated from outside of you. YOU hold the key to the box with the positive messages about yourself. USE IT! Open your mind to the willingness to say, "I am worthwhile. I AM willing to believe that. I AM making the decision to believe in myself. And I AM willing to do what it takes to be healthy-physically and emotionally."

You may need to have "talks" with anyone who gave you negative messages about yourself. Before you pass out with fear at the idea of confronting these people, take note: the "talks" do not have to be in person or with the real person at all! You can "talk" to these people by yourself… when you're in the car, taking a walk, sitting on the couch, hanging out in a deer stand, when in line at the grocery store…anytime and anywhere. You may choose to talk out loud (be prepared for people's reactions) OR you can "talk" to them inside your head. Just tell them what you think and how you feel about what they said or did to you… "I am furious that you repeatedly told me I would never amount to anything.

Do you know how hurtful those words were? Are you aware of the things I have never even bothered to try in my life because I kept hearing your voice in the back of my mind telling me I was worthless? I am so sad about all of the things I chose not to do. When I hear your voice in my head with those negative words I will tell you to 'BE QUIET' and I will make my own decisions about what I can and will do."

Trust me—you may have to have these sorts of "talks" frequently! This is not a one-time-will-fix-all sort of deal. You can also write letters to people who hurt you—but don't send them. Just write them to get your thoughts and feelings out of you! Burn the letters or "delete" them on your computer.

The other part in working through these old messages is to take an active role in making healthy decisions for yourself. You can only replace those past, negative messages by proving to yourself that you can make healthy decisions. Each time you follow through with a healthy decision, have a "talk" with yourself…*"Way to go!" "I'm doing great!" "It feels good to make healthy decisions for myself."*

95

Be patient. This is a process. Get professional help to work through these difficult issues. People often feel "disloyal" to parents when they talk "negatively" about them. You are not being disloyal to them. You are being loyal to yourself. Nor are you "blaming" them… you are simply stating facts about how you were treated and what impact that treatment has had on you. That is called holding a person accountable. Just like you are accountable for the decisions you make today. YOU are making the decisions for your life today and you are accountable for them, regardless of your past.

Heal your past and make each day a wonderful and healthy present!

HoMeWork
by APOD

Interacting With Your (Over)Reactions

Write down any times you are aware you have over-reacted to something in the past several weeks or months. Ask the people you trust the most if they are aware of any times they thought you overreacted to something in the past several weeks or months. Then answer the following questions related to those situations:

1. When have I felt like this in the past?

2. What was I able to do at that time to deal with my feelings in a healthy way?

3. Is it possible my present reaction may be coupled with my feelings of past situations where I may have felt similarly?

4. Is there anything I need to do to put closure on any situations from the past when I felt this way but did not/could not appropriately express my feelings? (journal, talk to the people involved, talk to a friend)

5. Is there a pattern to my way of reacting when I feel the way I did this time (and perhaps in similar situations in the past)?

6. What healthy ways can I deal with these situations and feelings in the future?

CORE SELF

" RECOVERY IS A WAY OF LIFE. IN ORDER TO BE ABLE TO FULLY EXPERIENCE THE BENEFITS OF LIFE IN RECOVERY, YOU NEED TO PEEL AWAY THE LAYERS OF THE ONION AND WORK TOWARD FINDING YOUR CORE SELF. "

97

– CONNIE STAPLETON, PH.D. (THRIVING!)

Q

Note from A Post-Op & A Doc: Because judging is such an important topic and because we get a lot of questions related to it, we decided to add a second question related to the prior one.

• • •

"*I find myself comparing my size to the size of other people. If they are smaller than I am, I decide they are 'better'.*

Why do I do this and how can I stop?"

99

THE POST-OP SAYS

Yesterday, the subject of "judgmentalism" came up in conversation (probably because I brought it up). Here's some context: I was talking about seeing people "belly up" to the all-you-can eat buffet and how it broke my heart. Someone made the statement that people who have lost weight can be harshly/negatively/unfairly judgmental of people who are currently obese in a sort of "us/them" mentality.

This is absolutely true. Human beings judge other human beings as a way of figuring out where they themselves fit in. The trouble begins when the judgment becomes a comparison of "I'm better/You're worse," as a way of making the "Judger" feel like they have the upper hand.

Of course, being judgmental is a complicated subject (one that The Doc really needs to address, but one which I will do my best to fairly discuss as a "civilian".) As always, I will explain it as my opinion and from my personal experience.

When I was morbidly obese, I always compared myself to others to see if I was the biggest person in the room, or if there was someone bigger. I also judged "skinny" people and concluded that they had no problems and lived perfect lives. I was a pretty vicious person and it only made me feel worse about myself. But, it was what I knew, so it's what I did.

As I began to lose weight, I continued to judge myself against others (under the pretext that I wanted to see where I fit in). Am I smaller than that person, or bigger? What does a size "X" look like? Oh my gosh, I'm so glad I'm not THAT big anymore. They could use Gastric Bypass!!! And so on.

And then, one day, I realized that what I was doing was destructive… to myself and to others. I realized that comparing myself to others, as I did, only made me feel worse about myself, and certainly didn't depict others in a positive way. It was a lose-lose proposition. It was like an addiction to me. I would say that I couldn't help myself…it's just what I did…it was harmless.

Only, it wasn't harmless - to me or anyone else. It was ugly and unhealthy. And so…I set about changing my behavior.

Whenever I said that I thought someone looked FAT and needed WLS - I would correct my thinking like this: "I know what it feels like to be obese, but I don't know their story and I don't know what it feels like to be them. Yes, I want them to understand healing, but WLS is not for everyone. They must be hurting, but I don't know their story, so I have no business judging them." And I'd let it go.

I did this A LOT.

I also did this with "skinny people." Every time I'd conclude that someone had it easy because they were thin (or that they were a "skinny bitch") -- I'd correct my thinking. I don't know their life and I don't know their physical circumstances. Maybe they can't gain weight but want to. Maybe they are in recovery from an eating disorder. Maybe they eat well and make healthy choices. Oh, there's something I hadn't considered -- but needed to.

That last statement took a while to really sink in, which is ironic, because…when I first lost weight, people started calling me a skinny bitch! They said I had it easy and didn't understand what it was like to struggle to lose weight. Interesting, isn't it? But that's how comparison and judgmentalism work.

Over time, I've worked hard to evaluate/assess others from a healthy standpoint -- as healthy as I can, given the fact that I am human and still prone to being snarky and critical at times.

The bottom line is, the terms "judgmental" and "critical" are often used interchangeably, but maybe there are slight differences. Maybe we have to look at including the words "comparing" and "discerning" in our thought process. We also have to remember that we "don't really know" anyone's story, so filling-in-the-blanks can be really unhealthy.

I'll leave you with this: If you've ever smoked and stopped, then you know ex-smokers have a reputation of being really judgmental. I'm an ex-smoker and I really do hate being around other smokers. Sadly, my daughter is a smoker, but she doesn't do it around me (which is good). I hope she'll stop because I think it's a rotten behavior. I justify my judgmentalism by saying, "Well, I was a smoker, so I can say these things because I stopped!" (Am I "better than" current smokers because I stopped? Do I justify my thinking because their smoking affects me? (The smoke gets in my nose and throat and makes me feel sick). Sounds suspiciously like unhealthy thinking to me...which is why I don't spend much time talking about smoking, ha ha. Okay, I don't think I have a "perfectly" healthy attitude about it. Yet.

Back to the subject at hand: Unhealthy judgmentalism and comparison usually only hurt the person doing the judging and comparing because (as that familiar saying goes), when you point your finger at someone, there are 3 fingers point back at you. It's true. So, I would encourage you to examine your behaviors. Do you criticize and condemn people to "make yourself look and feel better?" Do you write people off and decide they are "less-than" because they weigh more than you (or smoke? or have tattoos? have red hair?). If you do, you might want to work on that–for your own wellbeing.

THE DOC SAYS

I n part, because of the culture in which most of us were raised, we automatically "size ourselves up," in a comparative way. The natural tendency that follows is to make some sort of mental determination, or judgment. A judgment doesn't necessarily have to be a negative thing. I agree with Cari that we all need to make "judgments," in order to make decisions. A judgment can be a neutral statement just as easily as it can be a negative statement. Our connotation of the word "judgment," or "judgmental" is usually that it is a negative thing.

For example, I can look at another person and make the following (neutral, objective) determinations/judgments:

- She is taller than I am.
- She has blonde hair; I have brown.
- She dresses in a very classy way.
- She is overweight.
- She is underweight.
- She scored a 90 on her exam.

Notice that none of these statements have any sort of moral judgment associated with them. I believe it is moral judgment people assume when they hear the world judgment. Yet none of the above statements imply or even hint at moral judgment. They are observations, nothing more than objective judgments or statements. Notice especially numbers 2, 4 and 5. They make it clear that a judgment is an objective opinion; it is about employing discernment. I can look at a group of young adults who appear to be drunk, behaving raucously, swaying about, and slurring their words. Suppose they ask me to join them. My objective opinion, discernment, judgment is, "Those kids are drunk." My discernment is that I choose not to hang out with them, for a number of reasons. I'm a recovering alcoholic, so if they are drunk or using drugs, it wouldn't be wise for me to spend time hanging out with them. I'm in my 50's…hanging out with drunk teenagers is something I quit enjoying at least half my lifetime ago. Finally, I don't know these people; I'm not a very social person to begin with, so I'm not likely to hang out with many people, particularly those I don't know! I'm not making assumptions (moral judgments) about these people–in this example–I'm simply stating observations and my discernment (my choice) based on these observations.

The definition of judgment on **dictionary.com** is:

judg·ment [juhj-muh nt] *noun*
1. an act or instance of judging.
2. the ability to judge, make a decision, or form an opinion objectively, authoritatively, and wisely, especially in matters affecting action; good sense; discretion: a man of sound judgment.
3. the demonstration or exercise of such ability or capacity: The major was decorated for the judgment he showed under fire.
4. the forming of an opinion, estimate, notion, or conclusion, as from circumstances presented to the mind: Our judgment as to the cause of his failure must rest on the evidence.
5. the opinion formed: He regretted his hasty judgment.

Here's what we, as humans do with the statements above. We take an objective statement and apply a moral opinion/judgment on it, based on our own experiences, beliefs, and role models' experiences and beliefs. See what happens when we apply moral judgments to objective judgments:

She is taller than I am.
- *She's taller than me. I hate being short; people don't take me seriously.*
- *She's taller than me. I don't think I like her; just because she's tall, she thinks she can ignore me.*

She has blonde hair; I have brown.
- *She has blonde hair. Blonds attract men. I'm brunette, no wonder I don't have any guys interested in me.*
- *She's blonde–obviously dyed hair. She looks sleezy.*

She dresses in a very classy way.

- *She dresses classy. I would be intimidated to talk to her. I'm a down-home kind of gal. We wouldn't have anything in common.*
- *She dresses classy. I'll bet she's really smart.*

She is overweight.

- *She's overweight. She wouldn't be able to be our bookkeeper. What other applicants to we have?*
- *She's overweight. Even more than I am. She's gotta be more miserable than I am.*

She is underweight.

- *She's underweight. I wish I could look like that.*
- *She's underweight. She's obviously really mentally sick.*

She scored a 90 on her exam.

- *She scored 90! She thinks she's so much better than the rest of us.*
- *She scored 90! She must study all the time. I envy her.*

In the above statements, which start out as objective judgments (observations) became moral judgments by the person reporting. These moral judgments are not objective. They are based on comparison, self-depreciation, or, on the other hand, sometimes admiration. Either way, there are personal opinions infused with emotion imposed on what are, in and of themselves, neutral statements.

The way to stop comparing yourself, and making moral judgments based on neutral observations, is to become aware that you are doing so and then working to understand if doing so moves you to act in ways that lead toward or against your values–how you want to live. As usual, I'm going to say that this often requires therapy because it's difficult for us to dissect our own thoughts and behaviors.

HoMeWork
by APOD

HoMeWork
by APOD

List 10 ways you can think of off the top of your head that you typically judge others. THEN, be honest about what you feel insecure about, or superior about (neither of which is healthy) that leads to your making those judgments. Work on your own issues (or sweep your own side of the street, as they say in Recovery Circles) and stop comparing!

106

COMPARING

" WHEN YOU STOP COMPARING WHAT IS RIGHT HERE AND NOW WITH WHAT YOU WISH WERE, YOU CAN BEGIN TO ENJOY WHAT IS. "

– CHERI HUBER

Cari De La Cruz & Connie Stapleton, Ph.D.

Q

"I haven't had surgery yet. I really want to but I'm afraid I won't be able to keep the weight off. I've lost weight so many times before and of course, I always gained it back. I know a lot of other people have surgery and gain all of their weight back.

How can I conquer this fear?"

Cari De La Cruz & Connie Stapleton, Ph.D.

THE POST-OP SAYS

Have you ever overdrawn your checking account and been charged a fee because you didn't have enough money to cover the check? Why do they charge you money when you obviously don't have enough money in the first place? After all, you know that in order to open your account with the bank, and you have to agree to penalty fees, yet you still open the account. What about when you don't have enough money to buy a car, and need to get a loan? You actually have to prove that you don't need the money in order to get the best interest rate on the loan. That means if you have enough money to buy a car, you can pay less for the car, but if you can't afford the car, you're going to pay more for it…yet, you still buy the car. Let's try one more; say you want to have weight loss surgery. In order to qualify, most insurance companies and surgeons will require you to prove that you cannot successfully lose weight, which means, the more times you can prove you failed, the better!

Explain to me how proving you're a failure sets you up for success? How will a record of failure lead to a lifetime of success? Look, I'm not quibbling with insurance requirements, I'm just talking about the head stuff here, so don't get all worked up about surgical and insurance mandates, because they need a standard. But, back to the point: Repeated failure only proves that you have not yet succeeded. In other words, it doesn't mean you can't succeed, it just means you haven't succeeded yet. Are you shaking your head at me, saying I sound like some sort of rah-rah motivational guru? Well, I'm not–what I'm saying is, the very best thing for success is success and being successful at something helps you to become successful at something! I know it sounds obvious, but let's go with it and talk about that fear of failure after weight loss surgery. You have a long history of failure, and since that is the case, you're scratching your head and wondering what will make this time different? Do you think treating your obesity with surgery will guarantee that it works this time? Is it the idea that this is your last chance so the surgery has to work and that's why it will be different? The truth of the matter is, surgery won't magically change everything about your past and wipe the failure slate clean, so it's up to you to do the work of making changes in your thinking, attitude and behavior. This might sound overwhelming, causing you to wonder, "Where do I begin?" I suggest starting in the SELF-EFFICACY department. (I learned this one from The Doc, so I know it's true.) Many people believe they are abject failures in life because they can't seem to control that one, important part of their lives that everyone sees and judges them on: Their weight. Why can't I "just" control that "simple little" thing?...Why can't I lose weight and keep it off? Why can't I just put down the fork when I'm full? Sadly, the only conclusion some people draw is that they are failures at healthy weight management, and that is why they are failures in life.

BUT, does that mean they are failures at other things in life? I say, "no." If there's one thing I know, it's that MANY obese people are overachievers and perfectionists–meaning that–(since they just can't seem to get the weight thing right)–they work extra hard to be extra good at everything "else" in their lives. Does this sound familiar? Does it sound like you? Does it sound like a good thing or a bad thing?

Well, assuming you're in this position (probably a safe assumption), here's my objective opinion: If you have a job, then you must be pretty effective at being employed and earning money. If you have a roof over your head, then you must be pretty effective at taking care of your housing needs. If you have good friends, then you must be pretty effective at being a good friend. Do you see where I'm going with this? In order to establish self-efficacy at healthy weight management, you have to acknowledge that you are effective in other areas of your life, so you can prove that you really can succeed at something as significant as weight loss and weight management.

In my case, I began by sitting down and acknowledging things I did well. My list included things like: "I am a pretty good writer, I am artistic, I communicate well, I'm funny, I am a great employee, I work hard at doing my very best work, I'm a loving wife, daughter and mother, and a loyal friend." Next, I made a list of things I didn't typically do very well. That list included things like: "I am not a good athlete, I don't like to sweat, I don't journal well, I'm inconsistent with vitamins." The fact that I didn't do them well didn't mean I couldn't learn, and that is the key. I had to learn to do things well, and then do them.

So, to answer your question about how to get over the fear of failure about maintaining your weight loss, I suggest that you not start with being a success at weight loss at all. Start by making a list of things you do well. Then make a list of things you'd like to do better. Finally, make a list of your goals for living a healthy life after weight loss surgery. Consider things like losing weight so you can get off medication, move more easily, or be out of pain–those are great goals, but so are making healthier food choices, portioning/measuring food, getting support and/or therapy, and so on.

Now, start making those lists!

PS -- This isn't really "homework" because only The Doc can give HoMEWork... this is just work. That you might do at home. See? Big difference.

Things I do WELL

112

Things I 'd like to do BETTER

Goals for HEALTHY LIVING

THE DOC SAYS

I want to begin by congratulating you on being honest about your fear, which, I might add, can be a healthy fear. It's true that many people have weight loss surgery and re-gain their weight. This happens for a number of reasons. In fact, this is such a huge topic that we could write an entire book on this! *(Hey, Cari–let's make a note of that!)*

For now, let me list a few of the reasons for weight re-gain and then I am going to focus on one in particular, which I believe is common to many people who do re-gain some or all of their weight after WLS.

Common reasons people re-gain after WLS:

- *they weren't truly prepared to begin with (mentally and emotionally)*
- *they are resistant to following instructions by the physician and nutritionist*
- *they are going to do things their own way (which they did before surgery– and that didn't work so well)*
- *they falsely believe they can continue to eat "anything I want" after surgery, "but in smaller portions"*
- *they don't exercise regularly*
- *they "graze"*
- *they don't get help as soon as re-gain begins*
- *they lack support and do not seek it out on their own*
- *they subconsciously fear not being overweight or obese*
- *they lack self-efficacy (a belief that they can maintain weight loss)*

I'm sure we could come up with additional items to add to the list of why people re-gain their weight, but this gives you an overview. If you are a pre-op reading this book, then I would spend some time focusing on the first item in the list. In order to be truly prepared for WLS, look at the rest of the list and talk to someone about each of them! If you've already had WLS, you may be struggling with weight management (Cari and I like the words weight management much better than weight maintenance, but I'll let her explain that because she came up with it–and, as it usually is with Cari–it's brilliant)! If that is true for you, then you can also re-prepare by doing the same thing–talk with someone about your thoughts related to each of reasons listed regarding weight re-gain.

For now, I'm going to focus on the last item on the list above: a lack of self-efficacy. Addressing this issue requires (at least) a two-pronged approach. On one hand, you'll need to think about where your lack of self-efficacy (belief that you can do something) came from. On the other hand, you are going to have to work–yes work–as in capital W-O-R-K, on improving your belief that you can, and will, manage your weight at a healthy level for your body and age.

Let me explain...

I want to share a story with you. A patient once told me, "My mother said that when I was born into this world, her mother, my grandmother, said I was a cup. My mother thought her mother was loony, telling her I was a cup. As expected, she asked Grandma what that meant. Grandma said, that like every other child born into this world, I was born a full cup, a fully 'authentic person'. I was full of all of the 'good stuff' I would need to be happy in this world. I was full of love and kindness, joy and self-esteem, wonder and delight, compassion and generosity, faith and wisdom, and a belief in myself. My parents' job, Grandma said, was to not spill a single drop from my cup. What I've realized as I've gotten older, is that as I was growing up, more and more of my cup was spilled– some by my parents, some by mean kids at school, and some by complete strangers.

And then the worst thing of all happened. I started dumping it out myself. I called myself mean and hateful names like the ones the kids at school used to call me. I expected impossible things from myself. I stopped believing in myself. I stopped believing I was good and I stopped believing I could accomplish things I set out to do. As my self-esteem got lower and lower and my cup was getting more and more empty, the more I ate. I was trying to use food to fill the cup back up. What happened was...I got fat. I was no longer the person I was born into this world to be. I recently talked with mom about this and she reminded me that my 'authentic self' is still inside of me. She said she hoped I would try to find that person again."

That's a really powerful story. When I share it with people, along with examples of how our cups get spilled, they are able to identify some of the reasons they stopped believing in their ability to do things they want to do.

For so many WLS patients, losing weight, keeping weight off, and being "successful" at "dieting" has been something they've wanted to do for years and years and years. Even if they did lose weight, they "gained it back–plus some." This pattern, which results in re-gain teaches a person something–they can't trust their ability to get weight off and then manage it at a healthy level. The belief is "I CAN'T!" The belief is based on their past reality. And, as most of us have heard, past behaviors are the best predictors of future behaviors.

So long as you maintain a belief that you "can't" do something, whether it's a conscious or subconscious belief and as long as you continue to verbally berate yourself, whether it's out loud or to yourself, you will struggle mightily to follow through with healthy behaviors. This is low self-efficacy (your belief in your ability to do something). This translates, in the long run, to weight regain. The anecdote? Start saying, "I can" and "I will." Every single time you catch yourself insulting yourself, say STOP! And replace the negative thought with something more positive– even if you don't believe it at first. SO, "I blew it so why bother?" becomes "That was an unhealthy decision. I'll do better–starting right now." "I'm such an idiot" becomes "I made a mistake. I'll do better–starting right now." Negative self talk may be the greatest saboteur of sustained weight loss, so in order to keep that weight off permanently, start preparing now by using positive self-talk. Besides the weight loss surgery itself, learning and using positive self-talk may be the most powerful tool to help you permanently keep your weight off.

You don't need to have your emotional cup completely filled back up with self-love, self-worth and self-efficacy before you can choose grilled chicken on whole wheat rather than fried chicken on a white bun.

It is important that you work on filling your cup with increased self-efficacy, because it will get easier to maintain your healthy behaviors as you fill up. Why?

Listen to these two statements and see if one is more motivating than another...

1) "I have been shedding those extra, unwanted pounds. I feel so much healthier and am able to do so many things I've wanted to do. I'm glad I finally made the decision to treat myself with the loving care I know I'm worth."

Versus...

2) "I have been shedding these extra, unwanted pounds. I feel so much healthier and am able to do so many things I've wanted to do. I don't know why I think I'm going to keep it off this time. I've done this half a dozen times before and I know how it turns out in the end. Just like everything else I try and fail at..."

Obviously, the negative self-talk in the second statement is a set-up for failure. That's why changing your self-talk may be the most important thing you can do to keep your weight off...starting RIGHT NOW (in ADDITION, of course, to the Gotta Do Ems). Positive self-talk, whether you believe what you're telling yourself or not, makes a positive impact on your brain. How you think affects how you feel and how you feel affects how you behave. SO—one part of improving your self-efficacy is to change your self-talk and to give yourself positive feedback every time you make healthy decisions: "I'm proud of myself for going to the gym today." "I'm excited about choosing to have salmon today–what a great feeling!"

The other part in improving your self-efficacy is determining where the negative messages about your ability to do things came in the first place. Were you told you couldn't do something? Did teachers discourage you from trying things? Did other kids tease and shame you about something so you stopped trying? The reason this is important is so you realize you learned to think this way about yourself and you decided it was true. Of course you can't go and change the past. But you can change the present– for yourself. You can choose to accept that you were born with the ability to follow through. But only you can do it. Yes–others can encourage you, but it is ultimately up to you to believe you can make progress and only you that can make the healthy decisions for your life.

Developing self-efficacy and following through with healthy behaviors is just like weight loss...as A Post-Op & A Doc always say, "No one can do this for you–but you can't do it alone!"

Onward and forward, friends.

117

– Bonus Answer–

Post-Op here, explaining why I call it weight "management," instead of weight "maintenance". I have a love-hate relationship with words. Most of the time, I love them (especially the bigger ones), but sometimes, I really *don't* love them–especially words like: "perfection," "procrastination," "potential" and "maintenance." (Don't ask me why I seem to have a bigger problem with the "P" words, just go with it.) It's not that the words I dislike are bad; it's just that, my brain often interprets them differently than they were intended. For example, when someone says, "You can't eat that," I hear "Yes, I can. Don't tell me what I can't do." See? I have a problem with the word, "can't"...unless it's to excuse myself from having to do something I don't want to do (like exercise). In that case, the word "can't" comes in quite handy–at least it did for about 40 years–until I realized the power of the word, "can't." The day I learned that I "can't" use the word "can't" was the day I learned that substituting healthy words for words I deem to be "unhealthy" was a really great recovery tool.

For example, let's say there are chocolate cookies in my general vicinity and I need to convince myself to stay clear of them. If I tell myself that I "can't" eat chocolate chip cookies, I'll immediately tell myself, "I can TOO eat those chocolate cookies!" at which point I will eat chocolate cookies until they're all gone (and will still want more.) However, since I know that about myself, I can "choose" to use a different word like, "choose"–as in, "I choose not to eat those chocolate chip cookies.". If I don't like the word "choose," I might use the word "option," as in, "Those cookies just aren't an option for me." Make sense?

Great, so now you know that I talk to myself (and answer), but we weren't talking about my internal dialogues, The Doc asked me to explain why I use the word "management" instead of "maintenance." Maintenance is one of those words that I dislike due to a rather questionable history, (especially where weight is concerned.) In the past, whenever I'd "start" a new diet, the first thing I'd learn at the meeting (Weight Watchers, Jenny Craig, etc.) was: **MAINTENANCE.** Yes, the carrot cake on the stick was: "maintenance" –– that magical time "at the end" of my weight loss "punishment" where I'd get to "stop" doing whatever it was I was doing that got me to goal! In retrospect, it makes perfect sense, doesn't it? It doesn't? Well, that's the way it was always represented to me; **people on maintenance get to eat more things and have more freedom than people who are are NOT on maintenance.** (Are you concerned about my thought process, or are you thinking this sounds a tad familiar?)

Let me see if I can make this clearer: How about if I give an example of maintenance that doesn't have anything to do with diet or exercise: **Automobiles.** In the automotive world, cars require MAINTENANCE–regular, documented *maintenance.* When you buy a new car, it comes with a user's manual that has a "maintenance" section (just *after* the "Troubleshooting" section, and *before* the *"My hazard lights are blinking and I don't know how to turn them off"* chapter. Yes, there is a chapter devoted to questions like that. (FAQ's), which can only mean that not being able to find your hazard indicators is a frequently asked question. So, there.)

Remember that dodgy history I have with weight maintenance? As it turns out, the problem was even *worse* with automotive maintenance! Once I'd drive the car off the lot, that user's manual would get stuffed into the glove box...where it would remain (unopened and unread), until I sold the car. Don't get me wrong–I could have used it any time I wanted to–just by moving that big stack of napkins (from all of those drive-thru restaurant trips I made), a tire pressure gauge (that I didn't know how to use), the hub lock thingie (that I could never find when AAA came to change my tire), and my little portfolio with the registration and insurance card in it (that I could never find when I got pulled over. That one time.) Handy as ever... right there at my fingertips.

As you can see, my automotive maintenance record was spotty and denial of "maintenance" strong. But, this never became an issue until that mechanic asked me for my "oil change records" and proof that I'd had done the 25 and 50 thousand mile transmission servicing. Proof? Why should I have to prove I did the maintenance? Of course, I hadn't performed the required maintenance...anymore than I'd flossed my teeth after every meal (Dental Maintenance; another big problem.) Perhaps you're getting an inkling about why I hate the words "perfection, procrastination and potential." (or maybe you just think I have trouble with food, teeth and cars).

119

Whatever the case– to me, all of those words represent *impossible* goals, or goals I *missed* or *never tried* to achieve. **Maintenance** is just another one of those "yucky goal words," because maintenance always represented goals I missed, never achieved, or didn't even try to attain. Which brings us back to the original discussion at hand. Wanna know how I "managed" my problem with "maintenance"? I stopped using the word "MAINTENANCE" and started using the word "MANAGEMENT"! That's right! I promoted myself from head of maintenance to upper management -- with the substitution of a few letters and some new thoughts, feelings and behaviors.

Great idea, don't you think? The word "Management" has all sorts of positive connotations, including *"influence, responsibility, accountability, capabilitity, and continuity"*–all incredibly motivating "action" words that mean my health is *not a place in time, a number on the scale, or a desintation*. Management means my health is something I can CHOOSE to MANAGE and (just like my car), if I want my body to run well, I'll need to schedule regular service calls (annual check-ups), keep my fluids topped off (drink plenty of water), get tuned-up when necessary (have my blood drawn, adjust my vitamins), use quality gas (the best food and supplements I can afford), track my mileage (have an exercise log) and keep it clean (take pride in my appearance).

I just thought of another word: "Journal"...like in the back of the car manual where it says I have to change my oil every 6,000 miles and make sure the mechanic stamps and dates it. I hear you now, "It's a good thing I don't have a user's manual for my body!" Not so fast. You should know that "bariatric owner's manuals" (handbooks for healthy living after surgery) are available from the ASMBS, your bariatric nutritionist or surgeon's bariatric center of excellence office. And yes, if it's a good one, it will have checklists, places for journaling, and maintenance (management?) schedules.

I'll leave you with this: Whether you choose to "Maintain" a healthy weight and lifestyle, or you prefer to "Manage" it -- be sure you're using the words correctly. After all, if you think weight *maintenance* means you get to "stop doing whatever you were doing to get what you got," you might wanna change words.

Yes, I DO think you can manage it...

What's the Big Deal?

Next time someone suggests you are over-reacting to something that happens in the present, (after you get past defending yourself) think to yourself of other times in your life that you felt similarly to how you are feeling about the thing that has you upset in the present. It's likely you can think of a time (or times) from the past when you felt like you're feeling now. A possible reason for your present (over)reaction may be due to a cumulative effect of having experienced the same "core issue" at various times in your past.

For example, let's say your sister-in-law, someone you truly love, has teased you about your short haircut. She's a good person and doesn't have any malice behind her teasing, but you don't like it and asked her the last time she did it to please not comment about your short haircut because it hurts your feelings. Several months later, she again makes a passing remark after you just got your hair cut. Rather than saying to her, *"I know you don't mean to hurt my feelings when you talk about my short hair, but I need you to know that I am hurt and now angry because I've asked you in the past not to do that. You just did it again and I need you to know that I would really appreciate your not doing that."* THAT would have been appropriate. Instead, you come unglued. You yell at her; you cry; you storm out. When she comes to talk with you about what happened, you realize that when you were a child, your parents always had your hair cut very short and people often mistook you for a boy. Your current, very strong reaction, was tied to the past.

You'll be amazed at how often it is the case that you are reacting to past issues in the present! Work through your past issues that show up in your present life. You'll be able to work through potential problems with those close to you much more peacefully!

Cari De La Cruz & Connie Stapleton, Ph.D.

MENTAL FLOSS

" ADDRESSING EMOTIONAL AND MENTAL HEALTH ISSUES, BOTH PRE- AND POST-OPERATIVELY, CAN MEAN THE DIFFERENCE BETWEEN MAINTAINING WEIGHT LOSS OR EXPERIENCING WEIGHT REGAIN FOLLOWING SURGERY. "

– CONNIE STAPLETON, PH.D.

Q

"*I hate the way I look. I hate the way I feel. I hate being me. I hear I can't love other people until I love myself. I feel like I love my husband, but I can't seem to be able to say anything I love about myself. What can I do to learn to love myself so I can love him and others better?*"

THE POST-OP SAYS

When I was obese, I considered myself to be a pretty loving person. I tried to always say and do loving things for my family and friends so they would know that I loved them. I was a pretty good person...except for the fact that I really didn't like myself. But (to misquote a song): What's **self**-love got to do with it? I mean, if no one knew how I felt about *me*, then things should have been fine with *them*.

Only, they *weren't*...You see, when I was obese, I double-filtered every single thought and feeling before I said or did a single thing! I didn't blink without first passing the situation through two filters: A "Me filter" and a "You Filter"(which meant that "I" always came before "you", by the way.) At the time, this didn't seem strange because, I thought everybody "double-filtered" their thoughts and feelings. Why wouldn't they? Filtering things just makes sense because it eliminates imperfections–like bitterness, right?

Hmm...maybe I'd better explain how I double-filtered everything so you can understand what I'm talking about. Remember–I applied this process to absolutely every situation in my life...

Me Filter:

- What will others think of ME if I do or say this?
- What will others think of ME if I go here or wear that?
- I'm having a "fat" day, my husband can't possible find ME attractive?
- I can't go meet with that client, then they'll see ME and know that I'm not as skinny as I sound on the phone!
- I can't walk in late–everyone will look at ME.
- If I go pick-up my daughter at her friend's house, her Mom will see ME and wonder why I'm so fat.
- Everyone will see ME eating and know why my butt is so big.
- Don't include ME in that picture...I look huge.
- Don't hug ME or you'll be able to feel my fat rolls.

Me Filter. *Me. Me. Me. Me. Me.*

You Filter:

- What will YOU think of ME if I do or say this?
- What will YOU think of ME if I go there or wear that?
- How can YOU possibly find ME attractive?
- YOU were expecting ME to be much thinner, weren't you?
- YOU are looking at ME because I am late.
- YOU think I'm a bad mom because my daughter will grow up and be fat like ME.
- YOU are watching ME eat and think I deserve to be fat.
- YOU won't want ME in the picture with you...I'm huge.
- YOU want to hug ME, but you'll feel my fat rolls.

You Filter: *Me. Me. Me. Me. Me.*

You know what? That "Me" filter was about *me* and the "You" filter was about *me* too! I thought I was double-filtering for my own "protection," but I was really double-filtering for my own "perception." In other words, I was more worried about how *others perceived me* than I was about how *I perceived others*. Wow! Here I thought filtering was a good thing, but apparently, you can over-filter and lose the flavor. (See what I did there?)

Okay, okay, let me bring it back around: What does my filtering process have to do with your question about being able to love others if you hate yourself? Well, it seems to ME that if everything is all about YOU, then it can't be about anyone *BUT* YOU. I mean, if you are consumed by everything you don't like about *yourself*, it's kinda hard to consider what you do like (or love) about somebody *else*, don't you think?

So, how did I become a person who actually loves myself (which means I can love others?) Well, I started by changing my filtration process! First, I threw away my "ME-filter" (which was more of "Me-*First*-Filter" anyway) because it made everything bitter. I began to look at the things I didn't like about myself–which means I learned to accept the unfiltered truth. While that didn't always leave a good taste in my mouth, it did help me see what I needed to change.

For example: I was a very critical and judgmental person who loved to put other people down. I mostly did it through gossip, but also with "biting humor" (which, I thought made it okay, but didn't!) Obviously, I did this to make myself feel better, but I really only felt worse. So, to change that, whenever I found myself being critical (of myself or someone else), I'd stop and find something positive to say instead.

Here's another example: I was extremely self-absorbed. I worried (obsessed) about my hair, my face and how I looked. Now, I'm not going to tell you I don't still pay attention to that, but rather than being all-consumed and always seeing myself in a negative light (which used to be the case), I work to have a balanced attitude about appearance and focus on improving my behavior. So, instead of thinking about how I look, I find ways to genuinely compliment other people about how they look. Basically, before, I had bitter negativity brewing in my head, so I worked to replace it with...oh, I don't know, sweet positivi-tea. (Ouch, that hurt, I know).

126

Basically, over time, as I began to let go of the negativity, I found room for positivity, which made room for good feelings, happiness and love. It may sound oversimple, but there's no reason to make it harder than it is. After all, why do you think they add sugar to things that are bitter? To make them taste better, of course. Things that taste better are more enjoyable and people naturally want more of them. However, since we aren't talking about coffee (or baked goods) here, I'll leave you with this: To brew a better you, throw your "Me-Filter" in the trash, accept the unfiltered truth about you, and find ways to sweeten those bitter thoughts and behaviors that have been leaving a bad taste in your mouth. Oh, and don't be surprised if people start saying they "want" what you're having!

THE DOC SAYS

Let me tell you what I hate. I hate hearing you talk that way about yourself! Not in an angry hate kind of way, but in a very sad way. I don't know if you can't "love" someone else until you "love" yourself, but I will say that the love you have for your husband and others will probably look and feel differently after you've learned to love yourself.

How about we start with something less of a stretch than going from "I hate myself" to "I love myself." If we conceptualize love and hate as being the opposite ends of the continuum, that means there is a lot of space in between. It's sort of like losing 150 pounds. That is a lot of weight to lose and also the reason many people are discouraged at the prospect of doing it. It's a long ways to go. The fact is it comes off a pound at a time. So let's look at the many steps along the way from hate to love.

To make things simple, use this chart:

HATE	DISLIKE	APPRECIATION	LIKE	ENJOY	GRATITUDE	LOVE

I just made this up...there's nothing scientific about this. It's just for illustrative purposes. The point is, you might need to start identifying things about yourself and learning to categorize them differently. In fact, I'll bet you don't really "hate" everything about yourself now.

Let's start with physical attributes. Arms, legs, eyes, nose, ears, hair, hands, etc. Do you literally "hate" everything about each part of your body and the way you look? Can you at least acknowledge appreciation for the fact that your arms enable you to carry things, write things, pick up the phone to talk to people, do a job, etc.? I hope you can because there are a lot of people who would love to have two hands and two arms to use. Heck, you might even be able to jump way up the scale to gratitude for having two legs you can walk on! And how about two eyes you can actually use for seeing the beauty of a blue sky or the brilliance of a sunset? I've only got the use of one eye and I LOVE my one eye! I love that it works and I love that I can see my grandbaby's face and the faces of my children and the smiles that other people wear. I love that I can choose not to look at violent movies and I can choose not to look at other things I find ugly or offensive.

Moving on to character traits. Sense of humor, compassion, honesty, dependability, kindness, trusting, cooperative, affectionate–just to name a few. Google "list of character traits" and see where you would rate yourself using the above chart. If you're honest, I'm certain you would not "hate" yourself on every one of your traits. Maybe you enjoy being creative. Maybe you are grateful you are affectionate–even if it's with animals!

The point is, you most likely do not "hate" everything about yourself. So start with recognizing things you don't "hate."

Secondly, stop using the word "hate" in anything related to yourself. Even if you think you "hate" the way you look, stop saying it. There is enough research that says your brain is affected by your self-talk. So whether or not you mean it when you say it, start being more kind about yourself to yourself. Use the word "appreciate"...it's at least more positive! And our brain responds to positive words in positive ways. Literally. When we talk about ourselves in positive ways, we create chemicals in our bodies that actually make us feel better.

It's also true that you can "fake it til you make it." Pretend you like yourself. Tell yourself you are a person who enjoys self-improvement and you will become that. Tell yourself you appreciate your sense of humor and you'll find yourself using it more often–and therefore appreciating yourself more.

Here's a question I have for you. Do you enjoy "hating" yourself? Do you even want to change? You may be thinking, "Right, Doc. What sort of psychobabble are you pulling here?" Check it out–some people want to be miserable! Some people want to stay "stuck"–whether it's stuck "hating" themselves or remaining obese (in spite of saying otherwise). What does "hating" yourself do for you? How are you benefitting?

I'll give you some possible answers: Staying "stuck" is a whole heck of a lot easier than making the changes to start liking yourself! It most definitely is easier. If you're going to start liking yourself, you will have to do some WORK! Focusing on self-talk. Choosing more positive words. Catching yourself when you start talking negatively about yourself.

Why–you might even have to follow through with some behaviors to show that you do actually like yourself...positive things like take care of your body, use your positive attributes to help yourself and others. It's WORK, I'm telling you! If you continue to "hate" yourself, it's a great excuse not to have to change. You can go right on hating yourself and expect nothing out of yourself and no one else will likely expect anything of you either!

My last comments on this business of "loving" yourself and others. Define "love." Are you talking about the feeling? Which feeling? The in-a-new-relationship feeling of love? The settled-in, comfortable feeling of love? Are you talking about the verb love? To do kind and loving things for yourself?

Let me suggest you start with the latter...DO "love" for yourself. Treat yourself kindly. That means healthy. Don't go fill your belly with junk food because that is not loving behavior toward yourself. Loving yourself means feeding it healthy. It means exercising the body you were given in which to navigate your way through life. Loving yourself means talking to yourself kindly. It means washing your face and brushing your teeth at night. It means taking time to play and quiet time to reflect. Loving yourself means holding yourself accountable for your behavior. It means making the effort and doing the work to improve your life, both emotionally and physically. The feelings you have about yourself will follow the actions. When that husband you love treats you kindly, helps you out around the house, says loving words to you, touches you gently, and smiles at you, the feelings of love for him increase. It'll work the same way with yourself!

129

The Power of Love

Love as a Verb: Loving Myself

LOVING THE THINGS I DO (Leisure Activities)

When I have a great deal of time (several hours or longer), I enjoy:

1. _____

2. _____

3. _____

When I have an hour or less, I enjoy:

1. _____

2. _____

3. _____

Make an effort to note one way you showed love for yourself by engaging in some leisure activity you enjoy each day or week.

LOVING MYSELF (Accepting Compliments; Loving Self-Talk)

1. When someone gives you a compliment, simply say, THANK YOU.

2. When you find yourself mentally comparing yourself to another person, say to yourself, "KNOCK IT OFF!" Then tell yourself something positive about your own looks.

BODY+SOUL

" DISEASES OF THE SOUL ARE MORE DANGEROUS AND MORE NUMEROUS THAN THOSE OF THE BODY. "

– CICERO

Cari De La Cruz & Connie Stapleton, Ph.D.

Q

"I can't catch a break. I finally had surgery and it seems like so many things are working against me. The people at work want to sabotage me. They always bring sweets to the office. My husband complains if I leave to go to the gym so I can't work out. And I have to keep stuff in the house the kids like and bake cookies for their events at school.

How am I supposed to keep my weight off with everyone working against me?"

THE POST-OP SAYS

Oooh! I'm clapping my hands with glee because I get to answer this one, but don't expect it to be a rosy answer. Get ready for some hard truth: **When all you see is you, then everything will always be about you.**

What? Repeat after me (even if you don't believe it yet): ***This is not about me. This is not about me. This is not about me.*** Got it? Okay. Let me just rephrase what you said up there (just to be sure I understand):

- *You can't catch a break and nothing ever works out for you.*

- *You are the only person on the planet for whom the surgery did not work.*

- *People are sabotaging you by bringing foods other people like to eat.*

- *Your husband is shackling you to the sofa so you can't leave the house.*

- *You feed your children junk food that you've determined is not healthy for you, and then you bring it to school to make other children unhealthy. You have no healthy choices available to you.*

- *How can you be expected to do the right thing when everyone else is doing the wrong thing? It's not your fault. You're not responsible. It's them.*

That's weird…it sounds different when I say it. Almost…silly really. Like, the whole world wakes up every morning and conspires against you; as if they've signed up to be a part of a destructive plot to keep you fat! Doesn't that seem like a lot of work? Do you wake up every morning and plot ways to make other people's lives miserable? (If you do, we need to talk.) Do you spend every minute of the day imagining ways to make your kids and the kids at school sick? Do you honestly sit around and think about everyone else all day long?

Don't lie to me. You're thinking about yourself all day long, so you can't possibly be thinking about everyone else and…guess what? They're probably thinking about themselves too, so THEY can't be thinking about you. Too logical?

Let me break it down. All of that stuff up there is just one big blamestorm. You are not being accountable for your own crap and are choosing to point the finger at everyone else.

Ouch! That sounds mean, but it's not. It's firm and fair, and the sooner you realize that other people are not thinking about you as much as you think they are, the sooner you can begin thinking about yourself in healthier ways. You can start thinking things like, *"What can I bring to the office to share with everyone that we can all enjoy?" "If I don't feel strong enough to bake or buy cookies (or don't have a healthy, fun alternative), can I enlist the help of another mother to assist me in bringing something to the sale?" "Can I invite my husband to join me at the gym? Maybe he'll want to take a class with me or teach me how to lift some weights?" "What role do I play in my own health, and what can I do to ensure I manage my weight?"*

In the final analysis, when you stop making everything ***all about you*** (and accusing others of doing the same), you can begin inviting them to join you in healthy, balanced living. I say, put an end to those conspiracy theories and start planning your recovery.

135

THE DOC SAYS

If you said these exact words in an AA meeting, the response you would get would be this: "Poor me! Poor me! POUR ME ANOTHER DRINK!" It's rather sarcastic, but the point is a good one. Focusing on, and lamenting about all of these PITAs as I call them (PAINS IN THE ARSE), gives me an excuse to pour me another drink–because God knows with all that crap going on, a person needs to drink! Right? WRONG!

In the case of a person struggling with weight and/or food addiction, the response might be, *"Poor me! Poor me! POUR ME ANOTHER MILKSHAKE...or sweet tea, or sugar-filled soda."* The idea is the same. How can anyone expect me to make healthy food choices with all of this crap going on in my life?

Brace yourself...here comes the VERY FIRM (and yet, still fair) DOC!

Excuses, excuses, excuses. They are easy to find. *"There are food ads everywhere."* That's true–it's not an excuse to eat poorly. *"My life is filled with stress."* It may be. Eating poorly makes you feel worse and less able to deal with all that stress. *"I don't have time to exercise."* Who does? You'll have to replace something (TV, Facebook time, recipe reading time, phone call time) and fill that space with exercise. *"My family needs to have some snacks and treats at home."* BS. No, they don't. There are plenty of those to be had at school, sports events, work, and friends' houses. *"It's too expensive to eat healthy."* How much were you spending at the drive thru? On junk food? *"It's hard to do all of the things it takes to manage my weight."* Yep. Isn't having a healthy weight what you said you wanted?

I bristle at excuses. I lose patience very quickly with chronic excuses. In fact, if I've worked with a patient long enough and they truly know I care about them, when they start whining and giving me all sorts of excuses, I just look at them with no expression and say, "Wah. Wah. Wah." If I REALLY know them well and they REALLY know I care about them, I'll pick my sign that says GTFU. The ones who already knows what it means just chuckle. The first time, however, they'll say, "What does that mean?" I lean forward, look at them square in the face and say, "GROW THE FRICK UP!" OH MY! Yep, I really do.

Life ain't easy. And you don't HAVE to do many things if you choose not to. You don't have to run marathons. However, if you truly want to, you're gonna have to do a whole lot of W-O-R-K to accomplish that. It takes EFFORT! Personally, I have no desire to run a marathon, so I'm not going to do that work or put in that effort. I DO, however, want to keep my body healthy and at a healthy weight. That also requires effort and I AM willing to do that–because I genuinely want the desired outcome. You don't have to write a book. But if you want to, that, too, takes effort. I am, at this moment, NOT watching television, NOT hanging out with friends, NOT reading a relaxing novel, and NOT playing with my grandbaby–all things I enjoy doing. I AM making time to write, because I want the finished product.

Hey–you don't even HAVE to go to work! No, you don't! However, if you want the paycheck that going to work provides, then you go to work. Is it easy to go to work? Not for most people. Lots of people have to arrange for childcare to go to work. Everyone has to do something to get ready to go to work–even if you work at home. We WANT the desired outcome, so we find a way to make it to work.

I'm certain someone along the way informed you that managing a healthy lifestyle and healthy weight was going to require E-F-F-O-R-T. I suspect you realized that your life and the busy-ness of it and the people at work, and the rest of the world, for the most part–were going to maintain their own ways of doing things. If that meant there would still be donuts in the break room after you had WLS, then that's what it means. If you played taxi driver for your kids events before surgery, you're still doing it after. It takes EFFORT to adjust your own eating and exercise needs around the realities of your world. So either do it or don't. But, *don't* bring your excuses to this Doc!

Here's the FAIR part of me. I DO know it's hard. It's hard for me and everyone else to make time to exercise. It's of equal difficulty for me and for everyone to make the decision to put healthy food in our bodies and to forego the junk food that is nearly everywhere to be found. It takes everyone who prepares their own healthy food the same amount of time, regardless of what other things are going on in their lives. I DO know that some people have more to contend with than others and that it truly IS more difficult for some people than others. I am compassionate with myself and all of my patients about the difficulties they face in their lives. Rather than allow excuses, however, I work to help them find ways to "accept what they cannot change, change the things they can, and the wisdom to know the difference." (That's the serenity prayer.)

The reality is that if we want to make time to train for a marathon, if we want to take time to go back to college to get the job we've always wanted, if we want to take time to watch our favorite television shows, if we want to spend an hour on Facebook, if we want to get our paycheck, we do what it takes and we make the time.

Oh, and for the author of this question—we need to work on the stinkin' thinkin', as well. As we've discussed many times in this book—how we think and talk makes a big difference! One last thought—I would also suggest you consider if being a "victim" serves a purpose for you. I suspect it does, but that won't make your life any better! I promise

Excuse Me?

List your (5) five typical excuses you use to convince yourself you can't possibly do what is necessary for you to do in order to keep your weight at a healthy level. After each, write down what you will tell yourself in the future so you don't allow yourself to "get away with that."

139

1. _____

2. _____

3. _____

4. _____

5. _____

Cari De La Cruz & Connie Stapleton, Ph.D.

TRIUMPH

" CONSCIOUS CHOICE, BOLSTERED BY POSITIVE THINKING AND A REPERTOIRE OF NEW BEHAVIORAL SKILLS IS THE ONLY WAY TO TRIUMPH OVER YEARS OF NEGATIVE BEHAVIOR. "

– CONNIE STAPLETON, PH.D. (EAT IT UP!)

Q

"I had WLS 7 months ago and I really miss food. Since I can't eat the things I _love_ anymore, I watch the food channel and go to recipe sites to get ideas for healthy things I might actually _like_. But...sometimes when I'm on Facebook, I see photos of desserts and imagine myself eating everything on the plate! Unfortunately, I still have a long way to go to meet my goal, and the scale just isn't moving fast enough, so I guess I'll look at the food, instead of eating it.

Why didn't someone tell me I'd miss food so much?"

I don't know whether you miss the *actual* food or the *idea* of food, but one thing is for sure–weight loss surgery didn't change how you *feel* about food. If you've learned anything from hanging out with A Post-Op & A Doc, you know that morbidly obese people do not have a healthy relationship with food, and surgery doesn't fix that. On the contrary, surgery simply changes the rules of engagement, making it harder to spend "quality" time together.

The thing is, having surgery to fix a bad relationship with food is like your mom and dad forcing you to stop seeing that girlfriend or boyfriend because they aren't good for you. You still want to be with them, so maybe you even sneak off to see them, but it's not the same. Whenever you are together, you feel ashamed, guilty, sneaky and embarrassed. The worst part is, you can't tell anyone what you're doing, because they'll get mad and call you a cheater, so what are you supposed to do? Suddenly, you aren't "allowed" to spend time with the other half of your primary relationship, OR the people you and your food used to hang out with! It's like you got a divorce and all of your friends sided with with your ex! Since surgery, you're single and unable to have a healthy relationship with food...which doesn't stop the temptation, because food is EVERYWHERE.

Why do you suppose it's so hard to be around food after WLS? Maybe the bigger question is, why is it so hard to stay AWAY from food after WLS? C'mon, have you ever been to the food court at the local mall? If the smell of the Cinnabons didn't get you the instant you open the door, then the smell of all of the that food will! Each restaurant makes sure you can smell what they're cooking, there are yummy looking pictures of the dishes on the big menu behind the cashier, and everything they sell is on display, right there under the glass. It's quite tempting, especially with all those people giving you free samples from a tray. You don't have a problem with mall food?

Okay, ever been to Costco on a Saturday? I guarantee you cannot successfully run the grocery gauntlet from 75" flat screen TV's to 1000-sheet rolls of toilet paper without having to fend off at least 15 toothpick-impaled fried food choices, something from a VitaMix Blender, and about 10 desserts.

What is the deal? You're not there for the spring sausage or sushi rolls, yet you're inexplicably drawn to those little sample carts like silk to a zipper. You're helpless and cannot say "no," and those pizza pushers aren't helping. Why would they? They have a job to do—just like those people in Las Vegas shoving "GIRLS! GIRLS! GIRLS!" cards into your pocket, only in this case, they're ruthlessly (and indiscriminately) pushing chocolate cream canoles and coconut shrimp skewers on you, and you're feeling pretty attacked.

So, you stay home.

But, you can't get away from it there either, because you're recording at least two daily programs from each of the 43 satellite channels devoted entirely to food, your Facebook newsfeed is crawling with pictures of your friends posing with decadent desserts, and you're getting daily recipe emails from the top 10 food sites on the web! Hmmm....

What was the question again? Oh yeah, **you miss food and don't know why.** Well, I'm no expert, but I'm going to go out on a limb here and say that you're not doing yourself any favors by surrounding yourself with food at every turn. Perhaps, more importantly, since you never made peace with the food before you had surgery (by creating a healthy relationship), you're still fantacizing about it, and since you can't actually eat it...you surround yourself *by* it, immerse yourself *in* it, and try desperately to distract yourself *from* it. That, my friend is what we euphemistcally call "Food Porn," and believe me when I say, having a voyeuristic fling with cream filled cupcakes is no different than actually shoving them into your mouth.

Okay, I can hear you saying, "But, looking at pictures of cupcakes can't hurt me because there are zero calories in pictures." Well, I'll agree that pictures don't have calories, but I won't agree that looking at pictures of food won't hurt you, because what you're doing is "obsessing" over something you "can't have." To me, it doesn't make sense to focus on NOT eating something I shouldn't, because I'd rather spend time eating what I can. I kinda think it's the difference between marinating in misery or celebrating in recovery.

Cari De La Cruz & Connie Stapleton, Ph.D.

So, back to you and your sadness about missing food (and the friends that go with it), I would encourage you to stop obsessing about things like the food channel, recipe websites, and pictures of food—yes, even channels, websites and pictures with healthy food options, because even they can be unhealthy if you find yourself fixating on them. Start hanging out with people who share your commitment to healthy eating and living, and choose some healthy recipes that you like, will make, and can eat. Change the settings on your DVR to record Zumba or Yoga programming, and then invite a friend over so you can exercise together.

Ultimately, surgery changes the *amount and/or type of food* you can eat (health work); it doesn't change how you *think* or *feel* about those foods (head and heart work). That is up to you, and a great way to get help and develop a healthy relationship with yourself and food is to regularly attend support groups and get therapy if you need it. I can't tell you you need it... but I can tell you you could use it!

'm thinking about the actual terminology…"**food porn.**" I can't remember where or when I first heard this phrase, but I think it's the perfect choice of words to describe the obsession people have with food. Ironically, I'm certified as a sex addiction therapist…so I also work with sex addiction quite regularly. (In fact, as I write my response to this question, I'm on an airplane to attend a conference on sex addiction treatment, where I'm more than certain I will hear the word "porn" much more often than I'd actually like to! And I know I will be thinking of how that word applies to food as well as to sex…)

Pornography. What does that word connote for you? When you hear the words "porn," "porno," or "pornography" how do you feel? Some people say they immediately think "dirty," because they only heard the word in relation to "bad" sexual behavior and/or things ("dirty" magazines, "perverts," disgusting movies and sinful behaviors). They feel "disgusted," "nauseated," "ashamed," or "embarrassed." Sex addicts often feel shame and embarrassment because they believe they are doing something "wrong," either by thinking about pornography/sex and/or engaging in the use of it, even though they want to stop. Some people, when they hear those same words, "porn," "porno," or "pornography" admit (some sheepishly) that they feel excited because "those sorts of things" were off limits and were therefore appealing, or because they sound "naughty," which may add an element of curiosity. Some sex addicts experience anticipation just hearing the word "pornography" and some sex addicts experience both anticipation and shame in relation to pornography. Some people are neutral and couldn't care less about those "words," or any of the associated behaviors or *acoutraments*.

What do you think of when you hear the words "food porn?" How do you feel when you hear them? Are you struck with a sense of shame? A feeling of excitement? Do those words not mean anything because they simply don't resonate with who you are?

Let me talk about what Cari and I mean when we refer to "food porn" and say a few words on why we call it that.

145

When A Post-Op & A Doc say "food porn," we mean things such as:

- being pre-occupied with your weight (which is not the same as knowing how much you weigh),
- over-focusing on numbers (not the same as being aware):
  - clothing size
  - the number on the scale
  - calories
  - grams of protein, fat, sugar
  - comparing your numbers (weight, pounds lost, clothing size) with others
  - pre-occupation with recipes (that is not the same as selecting healthy recipes)
- mental obsession on food, weight and numbers (see above)
- continual "dieting" and discussions about "dieting" and "diets"
- focusing on other people's weight, food choices, etc. (kids, friends, strangers).

Think about it...in regard to these, and other examples of "food porn," which I hope our readers will share with us, many people feel "ashamed," "embarrassed," or "disgusted" with themselves. They know they are pre-occupied with food and know the constant focus on food is not healthy for them, as it often leads to engaging in over-eating or an unhealthy use of food. Oftentimes they truly wish they could escape the obsession of food and weight-related thoughts. Many people become excited by, or eagerly engaged in food porn. They welcome the distraction it brings and stay lost in the thoughts or behaviors related to food/eating for hours at a time. Some people feel both shame and enthusiasm when thinking about, or engaging in food and weight-related behaviors.

Hence, food porn.

For a sex addict, engaging in sexual pornography is often a trigger that leads to unhealthy sexual behaviors. For a food addict, engaging in food porn can similarly involve triggers that lead to engaging in unhealthy eating.

All people have needs related to sex and eating. Both are healthy and normal needs. Both sex and eating can be engaged in in ways that are unhealthy for a person–physically, emotionally and spiritually.

Engaging in healthy sexual behaviors is recommended for sex addicts. Eating in a healthy way is recommended for food addicts.

Engaging in sexual pornography is discouraged for sex addicts. Engaging in food porn is discouraged for food addicts.

Are all obese people food addicts? Not physically, although some are. Psychologically? I believe many obese people are, in fact, psychologically addicted to food.

I DIDN'T SAY ALL!!!!

Do you engage in food porn? Does it interfere with your healthy recovery from obesity? Is engaging in food porn simply a way to remain obsessed with food? Be honest with yourself. If you do engage in food porn and it prevents you from living a life in recovery from obesity, then please get help for it.

147

The bottom line of being obsessed with food and numbers related to food is this: Focusing on these things prevents us from having to deal with unpleasant thoughts, feelings, memories, and body sensations that we don't want to experience. While one spouse spends hours online reading recipes and other spends hours online watching naked people engage in naked people activities, both avoid dealing with their empty relationship. Get how it works?

One of my favorite recovery slogans is this: *There's no shame in being an addict. These IS shame in doing nothing about it.* Please do something about it…get help.

Need to Slip Into Something More Comfortable?

Make a list of things that your body can do now that you have lost excess weight that it couldn't do before you had weight loss surgery. Reflect on the joys of these things and read this list daily if necessary!

Write out your answers to the following questions:

1. What are all the ways I engage in food porn (feel free to add to this list as you notice new ways you *participate in the plethora of food porn proliferating* our planet...sorry, I just couldn't resist the alliteration!)

2. As you choose to let go of your engagement of food porn *(see how I just slipped that in there..."assuming the sale"–that's, what we called it back in my encyclopedia-selling days!)* notice how you feel when you no longer engage in it. Take a risk, go COLD TURKEY! *[Post-Op Here: COLD TURKEY? Pssst! Hey Doc, isn't this exercise meant to help them stop thinking about food?]* **NO FOOD PORN!** Do you have withdrawals (don't be surprised if you do)?! Do you find yourself engaging in other potentially unhealthy behaviors more frequently (shopping, smoking, drinking, etc.)? Are you moody, grumpy, tearful?

3. Get support as you let go of food porn. Talk about the process. Talk about how you're feeling. Talk about your awareness of how often you were engaging in food porn and what you are doing instead. Talk about the role that food played in your life. What do you need to deal with that food was keeping you away from?

FAMILY AFFAIR

" RECOVERY, LIKE OBESITY, IS A FAMILY AFFAIR! YOUR RECOVERY FROM OBESITY WILL BE ALL THE MORE JOYFUL IF YOUR FAMILY IS AN ACTIVE PART OF IT. "

– CONNIE STAPLETON, PH.D., (THRIVING!)

Cari De La Cruz & Connie Stapleton, Ph.D.

Q

" I've heard The Doc ask the question, '**What purpose does your weight serve?**' I don't understand what that means. Can you please explain?"

Okay, I'm not The Doc, so this is a tricky one to answer, but if I were to explain what it means to me, it would sound something like this: My obesity was the ultimate "Get Out of Jail Free" card. Ironic really, because obesity is a prison, but just go with it for a minute. In the game of Monopoly®, the Get Out of Jail Free (GOOJF) card lets you go about your business and keep doing whatever you were doing before. If you aren't in jail when you draw the card, you can keep the card (for future imprisonment) or sell it. As an aside, I never sold the GOOJF card when I played Monopoly, probably because I kept getting the *"Go Directly to Jail. Do Not Pass Go, Do Not Collect $200"* card, but I digress. The point is, when you play that card, you don't have to change anything about what you're doing. Some people have argued that Weight Loss Surgery is a "GOOJF" card and, to some degree, they might be right–especially on the emotional front. After all, are you required to change your emotional health in order to lose a single pound after weight loss surgery? Both sides could be argued, but on the face of it, I'd say "No." Which brings me back to my obesity and my personal GOOJF card.

When I played the obesity card, it meant that I didn't have to do certain things. I didn't have to help set up camp because I couldn't bend up and down and lift heavy things (bad back, bad knees). I didn't have to go get something from the motor home because I might fall climbing up or climbing down, so I'd have someone else do it (mostly because I did fall out of the motorhome...twice). I didn't have to go on hikes with everyone else because I needed to stay behind and get dinner ready. After all, I'd just slow everybody down. At home, I couldn't vacuum or make the bed (too heavy and I might throw my back out). And on and on...

In retrospect, I got "out" of a whole lot of things...but that GOOJF card was really a *Go Directly to Jail* card, because my obesity kept me from doing things–it didn't protect me from doing things. That was a lie I made up to... protect myself. So, what purpose did my obesity serve? I believe it gave me *excuses*. I had a GOOJF card that said I didn't have to show up for life and be responsible, and in the end, my obesity took away my freedom. Just like that game of Monopoly, I nearly went bankrupt paying the high price of living large; fortunately, weight loss surgery was my last pass at "Go" and I'm happy to report, I never looked back.

Now, who's up for a rousing game of LIFE®?

Purpose…When I ask the question, *"What purpose does your weight serve?"* a lot of people are confused. I too, was confused when I was asked questions like, *"Connie, what purpose does your anger serve?"* and *"Connie, what purpose has your working 80 hours a week served you?"* and *"Connie, what purpose did those cigarettes serve you?"* and *"Connie, what purpose did all the drinking and the abuse of prescription medication serve you?"* Let me tell you, all of these questions came at me for weeks on end when I went through an outpatient treatment program in my late 20's (before going back to school to become "The Doc.") The truth is, my inappropriate use of anger, smoking cigarettes, my overabundant use of alcohol and narcotic pain medication, and my excessive working all served pretty much the same purposes: 1) to help me escape the realities of dealing effectively with adult life, which I felt unequipped to do, 2) to help me avoid many feelings I did not want to admit to myself and which I definitely did not want to experience (sadness, fear, disappointment, shame, guilt, inadequacy, and embarrassment), and 3) to provide me a false sense of "fitting in" somewhere.

Like me, you are probably saying something to yourself in the form of protective protest to what I've just written, such as, *"Oh My…I feel sad for her. I'm so glad I don't/haven't felt that way about myself or my life."* When I first entered treatment, I literally made an appointment with the counselor after the first two days and told her, *"Listen, I don't belong here with this group of people. My God! Some of them have been to jail, others were locked in closets when they were children, and there are people out there who don't even have several of their teeth! I've graduated from college. I have a husband who loves me and children I adore. I just don't have anything in common with these people."* You see, I didn't want to admit that I was like all of those people in so many ways. I was being horribly judgmental because I was afraid to recognize and admit that regardless of our external circumstances, underneath our addictions we all felt so much the same way. We all felt shame, guilt, fear, out of control, and sad, and I suspect you do, too (whether or not you are ready or willing to admit it.)

154

My feelings were not all related to my overt behaviors. Some were, of course. I was ashamed that I embarrassed myself (and others) when I drank. I was scared because I didn't have the "off" switch that normal drinkers have. I was ashamed of many things I did when I was drunk. I was embarrassed that I was a college graduate with a husband and three beautiful young children and my life was out of control. I was sad and scared because I knew that if I didn't stay in treatment and face whatever realities and feelings I was running from by working excessive hours, by using alcohol and drugs that I would need to keep using or find another way to numb myself.

Did food help you remain numb? Did focusing on the scale, a diet, the number of calories in food, spending a lot of time reading cookbooks and pouring over recipes, and obsessing about what you were going to eat next help you avoid something: troubles in a relationship? issues with extended family? having to work outside the home, face people and/or take a look at how you felt about your abilities? experiencing feelings that may surface if you weren't obsessed or pre-occupied with food-and-weight-related issues?

My belief is that food/weight did (and maybe still does?) serve one or more of those purposes for you. I also believe you may not be ready to accept that yet. However, I suspect that most people who struggle with obesity (if a medical issue was not the sole reason) do, indeed, use food for a purpose. Some of the "purposes" the WLS patients I have worked with will tell me food and weight have served for them include:

My weight allowed me to stay at home most of the time and therefore not have to deal with a lot of people.

- *I didn't want to deal with people because I was embarrassed and ashamed of how I looked.*
- *I didn't want to deal with people because I felt incompetent as an adult.*
- *I didn't want to deal with people because I am exceptionally shy and didn't know how to work through that.*
- *I didn't want to deal with people because I felt like a failure.*

Food was a friend to me…

- *when I was home alone as a child.*
- *when I was afraid.*
- *when I was deprived of anything sweet by my parents.*

Food became a symbol to me that I would never have to go without it as an adult because I often had to go without enough of it as a child.

My weight gave me "an excuse" not to deal with the opposite sex.

- *I didn't want to deal with the opposite sex because I have been abused by the opposite sex.*
- *I didn't want to deal with the opposite sex so no one would look at or approach me in a sexual way.*
- *I didn't want to deal with the opposite sex because I was told no one would ever want me and I knew if I was fat I wouldn't have to risk being rejected for my personality.*

My weight helped me reinforce the message that I would never amount to anything.

My weight helped me reinforce the message I was ugly.

My weight has been a way to punish myself.

- *I felt I deserved to be punished because my dad left when I was five. If I hadn't been a burden like my mom said, he would have stayed.*
- *I felt I deserved to be punished because the kids at school all hated me and I hated myself, too.*

My weight helped me avoid intimacy (physical/emotional) in relationships.

- *If I remained obese, my partner was less interested in sex.*
- *If I remained obese, I could tell my partner I was unable to have sex.*
- *If I remained obese, I could stay home and avoid having friendships.*
- *If I remained obese, I could focus on diets with my overweight friends and family members; that way, we didn't have to talk to about "real" things.*
- *If I remained obese, I had an excuse not to have to go to my kids' events where I felt uncomfortable around other adults.*

The list could go on. Regardless, if a person has lost and regained weight, then I believe their weight must serve some purpose, particularly if they adamantly claim they desperately want to be at a healthy weight AND if a medical cause is not the reason for their obesity.

If you're not quite there yet...not ready to acknowledge what purpose obesity or food played/plays for you, it's all right! Recovery From Obesity is a process. Learning to live fully—without the need for escapes from reality—takes time. And willingness. And effort. As long as you have those things, you'll come to realize, in time, what purpose your obesity has served you.

When you do come to terms with the fact that food has served important protective purposes for you, GET INTO THERAPY to deal with those issues and to learn healthy ways to deal with life issues. Otherwise, you are susceptible to remaining a slave to food, and also risk vulnerability to other means of escape from unwanted thoughts, feelings, sensations and experiences.

157

HoMeWork
by APOD

Do It On Purpose

Time to be brutally honest with yourself and write down what purpose(s) food and weight have served for you. Continue to add to this list as you think of more ways this fits for you. Be sure to remind yourself that as you learn to live in Recovery From Obesity you won't need food or your weight to protect you from anything; you no longer need it and can deal with life directly now.

BOUNDARIES

" BE PREPARED FOR PERSONAL AND SOCIAL RELATIONSHIPS TO CHANGE AFTER YOU HAVE WEIGHT LOSS SURGERY, AND ESPECIALLY AS YOU BEGIN TO IMPLEMENT NEW PERSONAL BOUNDARIES. "

– CONNIE STAPLETON, PH.D.

159

Cari De La Cruz & Connie Stapleton, Ph.D.

Q

"I hate it that other people criticize me for being overweight. I wish I were one of those people that could just eat whatever they want. Those skinny bitches don't have any idea what it's like to walk in my shoes.

How can I get other people to have more compassion?"

Hey! I'm a skinny bitch now, and guess what? I can't eat whatever I want...and neither can they. Trust me, anyone who says they can eat anything they want probably only eats carrots anyway. But, seriously, the first thing I would say is, whatever you think you know about someone else's metabolism probably isn't true, and the second thing is, even if it is true, what business is it of yours? Keep your eyes on your own paper! Who cares what they can or can't do? Do you have control over them? Do you have control over you?

Ah, now we are getting somewhere. You're worried about what someone else gets to do. Let me think about this for a second...I'm the baby sister. My brother is 4-years older than I, so when we were growing up, he got to do everything first. I mean *everything*. Mostly, because he's older, but also because he's a boy and...uh...didn't always make the best choices anyway, (but that's a discussion for another book) but, the point is, I can clearly remember whining to my parents about how "he" got to do everything first! Why couldn't I stay out late? (I implored) Why couldn't I go to that concert? (I begged.) Why is his curfew 1 a.m.? (I complained) And so on. He got to do *everything*. And so did (apparently) *everyone else in my world* because they "got" to do what I wanted to do, and I *couldn't*.

The funny thing is, the fact that my older brother did everything first didn't change a single thing for me. I was still the baby sister, I was still a girl, and I still wasn't allowed to do the things other people got to do. Guess what? I also couldn't run the 50-yard dash in under 8 seconds, I couldn't do a single chin-up, I wasn't able to swing on the rings or cross the monkey bars, and I definitely couldn't jump from the top of the Jungle Jim. So, you see, there were many things I *couldn't* do that others *could* do.

My recovery began the day I came to terms with the fact that there are some things you don't get to do, can't do or shouldn't do. That's life. Maybe you don't get to do it because you're too young (shave), maybe you can't do it because you're the wrong gender (childbirth), maybe you just *shouldn't* do it because it's a bad idea (crank call the Vatican).

Whatever the case, there are things you're not going to do. But, there are some things you **can** do, *if you're willing to work at it.*

Being healthy is one of those things.

Here's the truth: You're never too young, you're never the wrong gender, and it's never a bad idea to be healthy. Yes, I said never. And, regardless of whether *other* people make being healthy look easy, *you still have to do it*; regardless of whether other people think *I* make being healthy look easy, *I still have to do it*; heck, even if I make it look hard, you *still have to do it and so do I!* Basically, if you want what you say YOU want...you have to do it, regardless of what other people think. Why? Because ultimately, what others think or don't think...do or can't do, doesn't change the reality of what you CAN think *and* CAN do. Wanna know a secret? I happen to think you CAN do it, but I wouldn't worry about what I think...

Oh, as far as others having compassion for your struggles? Since I'm pretty sure you don't know what it's like to walk in their shoes either, why don't you put on your own shoes and have some compassion for *them*? By the way, you should start with some sensible shoes that don't pinch... compassion isn't always as easy as you *think* it should be.

163

Ah! This is definitely one of my favorite questions. It's almost weekly that I hear a patient talk about how "those skinny people JUDGE" the obese person...Is anyone picking up the double standard here? Is there not judgment going on by "skinny people" who criticize and make assumptions about the obese person...AND by the obese person who is similarly criticizing and making assumptions about the skinny person? I would say that there is...

In my post-op therapy groups for WLS patients, it's almost inevitable that I hear critical, judgmental and assumptive comments (judgments, actually) about people with other issues, problems or addictions. I actually welcome these because they provide such an opportunity for learning. Obese people, with good reason, don't like to be judged, criticized or have assumptions made about them (they're lazy, stupid, etc.). When one of the WLS patients comments about how irresponsible it is that anyone would overspend to the point where their home is up for foreclosure, or gamble to the point they are embezzling from their company, or an alcoholic doesn't "just push away from the bar," I remind them how it feels to them when people make judgments and assumptions about them, based on no more information than their size.

Do other people need to have more compassion and understanding toward the obese? BY ALL MEANS, YES! And obese people have to have more compassion toward others, as well. Therefore, the need for greater understanding, less judging and increased compassion is universal.

"Yeah, Doc, but people don't need to gamble. People don't need alcohol to live. But people DO need food." In terms of physiological survival, those are true statements. But that's as far as that EXCUSE can be played. People do NOT need sugar-filled foods, simple carbohydrate-filled foods, and fried foods in order to live. Junk food is not a necessity for survival. And if you're honest, the majority of obese people eat more than a "little bit" of junk food.

"Ummmm...Doc! What if those foods are all a person can afford?" IF, and I do mean IF that were truly that case, then I would consider that...I believe that for some families in this country, as some times in the history of this country, feeding one's family on inexpensive, filler foods may have been somewhat of a necessity. In RARE cases today, do I believe that is a LEGITIMATE reason for eating unhealthy foods.

In order for me to give credence to a person's needing to literally survive off of inexpensive filler foods such as rice, pasta, white bread and white potatoes, I would first need to be convinced they weren't eating at fast food joints or other restaurants, were not splurging on expensive cell phones and other electronic toys, spending money on cable television, and purchasing unessential things like expensive handbags. In my experience, in over ten years of working with WLS patients, many people are presently spending money on unnecessary luxuries when they could use that money to eat healthier food. (I told you I don't do well with excuses...). I AM FAIR, however, and willing to look at each person's situation. And I do agree that many non-nutritional foods are less expensive than some of the healthier foods. However, there are a number of articles written about how to eat healthy on a budget, so if that is an issue for you, then I recommend putting forth the effort to find those articles. If you are arguing that you don't have a computer, then go to the library or ask a friend to go for you and ask the librarian to get them some articles. OR ask the nutritionist at your WLS center to get you information on how to eat healthy on a budget!

Oh—and as for those "skinny bitches" being able to eat whatever they want...that's not very often the case. Just like it's not very often the case that a person is obese without eating too much unhealthy food and not exercising. That does happen, just like there are people who truly can eat how much of whatever they want and not gain weight. But the truth is, most "skinny bitches" are either under the age of 18 or they put effort into remaining at a healthy weight. Most healthy weight people choose what they eat very carefully and most get some degree of exercise. So again, be careful about judging others and making assumptions, keeping in mind how much you despise it.

Back to the last part of this question—"How can I get other people to have more compassion?" Educate them—in a kind way. Let them know that being obese does not mean one is "lazy, unmotivated, or stupid." Help them to understand that there are numerous, overlapping factors that lead to obesity including medical issues, medications, genetics, learned behaviors, and yes, personal eating behaviors. Invite others to get involved in educating the community about the realities of obesity. Encourage them to participate in healthy community activities–to organize or participate in group walks and to see the many obese people who are actively working to fight their obesity. Encourage others to provide support and encouragement to those who struggle with weight rather than criticize and condemn them. (Oh–and then do the same yourself...go to a Gambler's Anonymous meeting and listen to the struggles and triumphs those who suffer from that affliction deal with. Talk to an anorexic and hear how she battles many of the same demons that obese people fight...obsession with food, the scale, clothing size, calories, self-esteem and self-loathing, perfectionism and shame.)

166 Judging others, criticizing others, and making assumptions about others come too easily to all of us. Looking at ourselves and our own issues...much more difficult, but a whole hell of a lot more productive!

Judgment Call

In your heart of hearts, you know in what ways you are judgmental. Write down or talk to a friend or pray or send your thoughts out into the universe about the ways in which you are or have been judgmental toward others (specific groups, gossip, etc.). Make a conscious decision to remember that, like you, every other person comes from a place you are unaware of. Each person is the way they are based on events you know nothing about. Keep the focus on your own life and making the best choices you can for yourself and for those whose lives intersect with yours. Remember how much you dislike being judged for your weight or any other reason…and refrain from doing the same to others.

CRITICISM

" CRITICISM IS THE ART OF APPRAISING
OTHERS AT ONE'S OWN VALUE. "

– GEORGE JEAN NATHAN

Q

" I didn't realize before having weight loss surgery, just how much different everything would be. I knew my eating habits would have to change, but I had no idea that living as a healthy post-op would completely consume my life!"

JOB OPENING: Hours: M-F 24/7. No vacation pay. No sick days.
No experience required, but must be willing to learn on the job.

If you saw that employment ad, would you apply for the job? Most of us would say no...but what if the job opening was for...MARRIAGE? Let's say you would be applying to be a wife or husband? Would you take the job?

What if the job opening was for PARENTHOOD? You'd be applying for mother or father. Will you sign on the dotted line?

Those two "jobs"-livelihoods—fit the job description above, right? You don't get days off from being a mom, dad or spouse—not if you want your relationship to be healthy, anyway. You have to show up every day—whether you feel like it or not.

Well, guess what? I accepted that job as a spouse and as a mother. I accepted it again in 2007 when I decided to live in Recovery From Obesity. Oh, I didn't know it at the time, but living healthy is a full-time job. The benefits are incredible—so amazing, I can't even list them in the ad above—but, those benefits come with responsibilities, because being healthy is a JOB. Being healthy doesn't just happen. You have to show up and do the work. You don't get to "take a break" because you're tired and you don't get any sick days. If you're sick, you still need to take care of yourself.

Are you treating your obesity like a full-time job, or a hobby?

ON-THE-JOB TRAINING: Recovery From Obesity is a full-time job. If we are (or were) morbidly obese, then doesn't it stand to reason that we aren't (or weren't) doing a very good job of doing our job? Why do you suppose that is and what would an employer do if we did a poor job of doing our job?

Some places might fire you, but since you can't really be fired from being YOU (don't argue with me on this one), the only *real* option is ON-THE-JOB TRAINING. In other words, to do a better job of doing your job, you need solid instruction on healthy living, eating and thinking.

Oh, but I've got news for you...this instruction is going to require a whole lot more than just a single visit to a nutritionist, a stop over at a support group meeting, a session with a surgeon and a 1-hour psych-eval. Yeah. A LOT MORE.

It might take a solid year of working with a life coach or personal trainer. It might take regular attendance at 12-Step meetings. It might take annual attendance at educational conferences, targeted toward living fully in Recovery From Obesity. It might take 3-5 years of therapy (I vote "highly likely" on this one)…Heck, It might take ALL of these things, and more.

THINK ABOUT IT: In the past, most of us (raises hand here) did a horrible job at managing a healthy weight…so bad, in fact, that an employer would have fired us on the spot—so the idea that we would somehow magically be able to perform our job better (just by having weight loss surgery, or starting a diet), seems a bit…far-fetched. Don't you think?

My take on it is, to live fully in Recovery From Obesity, we need regular and ongoing ON-THE-JOB TRAINING. In my case, I'd like a certificate, suitable for framing or, at the very least, a 90-Day chip from OA and a smiley face on my lab results. (I'm not asking much).

171

You might decide that you want something different, but whatever ON-THE-JOB TRAINING you choose, understand that it takes effort and investment (of both time and money) to gain the tools you need to be healthy.

What sorts of educational "training" programs are you involved with to aide your "job performance" in Recovery From Obesity?

THE DOC SAYS

I love the analogies Cari gave about marriage, parenting and healthy living being full time jobs! I'm thinking they are all full time jobs in the the BIG full time job called life! Guess that makes us all great multi-taskers. If you never considered yourself to be very good at multi-tasking, I'm betting in just a few minutes you may think otherwise.

We're all currently living, which for the vast majority of us, means we are involved in all sorts of things...work, classes, children, grandchildren, immediate family, extended family, hobbies, sports, church, spouse, and, of course, taking care of our health! As Cari said, most of these activities could easily be described in terms of full time jobs. Yet somehow, as time goes by and we add new events and people into our lives, without the benefit of any additional hours in each day, we incorporate things into our busy lives without having to literally devote full time hours to each different group or activity. How do we do it? And what is the point I'm trying to make?!

The point I'm eventually going to get to is this... even though it seems like committing to Recovery From Obesity seems to take all of our time and energy (as though it was a full time job)–like other things in our lives, living a healthy lifestyle does eventually become a way of life that no longer requires our full conscious attention every single minute of the day.

Think back to when you started a particularly difficult job that required you to learn a number of new tasks. Let's say the job is night clerk at a hotel and you have never worked in that field (I haven't either, so I'm making things up here...). You'll need to learn how to schedule reservations over the phone, the procedure for checking guests into and out of the hotel, the protocol related to end-of-day accounting procedures, what to do in case of belligerent guests, what to do in case of threatening weather, and a host of other job duties. At first you make lists of what needs to be done when, you post sticky notes around the sides of the computer to remember important details related to booking rooms, you ask your co-worker what seems like a question every five minutes, and spend the first several weeks wondering how you will every remember the policies, protocols and procedures necessary to do your job well.

Within a matter of months, there are no sticky notes to be seen. You are making suggestions to improve procedures, and you are ready to train new employees.

When it comes to learning how to live a healthy lifestyle in Recovery From Obesity, the same ideas can be applied. All of a sudden, you have several different vitamins you need to take, some that need to be taken with food, others that need to be taken on an empty stomach, and some that must be taken a certain number of minutes after others. Oh, yeah– and some of the vitamins must be taken multiple times a day. You think you'll never remember just this part of the health care regimen.

Add to that the number of protein grams you need in a day. Keep in mind the maximum grams of simple carbohydrates and sugar you should have, and remember that the fiber count in food actually changes something about the carb count (which reminds you that you never were very good with numbers so perhaps you need to sign up for a math class...)!

173

Part of the healthy living lifestyle is making time for exercise...and that means more days of the week than not. Now you've got to rearrange dinner time, babysitting schedules, carpools and work hours. Lest we forget the food part of living in Recovery From Obesity, there are menus to plan, shopping to be done, and maintaining records of every morsel than one eats.

Remember starting the new job as night desk clerk? There were so many things to learn at once. You did what you needed to do in order to complete each task each day. You asked questions about things you didn't fully understand and you may even have asked for help during particularly busy or difficult times. In just a few months, you had learned most of the duties so well they barely required conscious effort.

That's how you develop a life of Recovery From Obesity. Make lists if you need to. Schedule your time. Write out your menus. Keep track of how many ounces of water and grams of protein you consume in a day. Leave sticky notes reminding you when to take which vitamins. Ask questions and ask for help when you need to.

In a matter of months, if you are diligent about following the instructions you are given from the start, you will be living a healthy lifestyle in short order! A full-time job gets assimilated into the bigger picture called LIFE! And the longer you keep up with the post-op protocol, the longer you'll get to enjoy a longer, fuller life!

Your Full-Time Jobs in Life

List all of your "roles," being sure to include Post-Op. Write down as many of the duties as you can think of related to each role. Then give yourself a huge round of applause for being one heck of an incredible multi-tasker! Pick one of the roles you listed and think about when you started that role. Perhaps all of the duties seemed overwhelming when you first became a "spouse" or a "parent" or an "engineer" or an "administrative assistant." Somehow you have managed to incorporate them all into your life and don't have to spend most of your time thinking about each and every one of them. From time to time, go through this mental exercise to realize that you have accomplished a number of roles and have learned to do so without constant thought about what to do and when to do it. You can do the same with your Recovery From Obesity!

EASY

" OBESITY ISN'T EASY. WHY WOULD
RECOVERY FROM OBESITY
BE ANY EASIER? "

– CARI DE LA CRUZ (THE POST-OP)

Q

" Some days I just don't feel very empassioned about doing the things I need to do to stay at a healthy weight. I know I signed up for eating healthy and making sure I exercise when I decided to have weight loss surgery, but sometimes I don't feel enthusiastic about actually doing those things like I thought I would.

What can I do to be more excited about following through with my healthy behaviors?"

> *"Don't follow your passion;*
> *bring your passion with you."*
>
> ~ *Mike Rowe (The Dirty Jobs guy)*

heard that comment and realized it was very much like what I'd been thinking about recently. It's good to be passionate about what you're doing (The Doc and I sure are!)–but what if you're doing a job that you aren't really passionate about...and you can't change your circumstances right now?

That's when I say, "bring your passion with you." Same with Recovery From Obesity. Some days, I don't feel very excited about making healthy choices. That's when I need to dig deep and find passion–which really means "living fully." Really living life–that's what matters to me, and I can certainly bring that passion to my Recovery.

I can also bring that passion to my day job...which, trust me, doesn't change the world, but does pay the bills, which are a reality in life. Even though I don't have a tremendous amount of passion about the work that I do at my "day job," I can help change someone else's world, even if it's in some small way. Helping them feel better for even a little while today, or helping them to produce a really great product that makes them feel good about their work. In other words, I can find ways to be passionate about what I'm doing, even when what I'm doing is not my passion.

Hmmm. This question makes me chuckle. I'll say a few words about what I find humorous, but think I'll just include an article that Cari and I wrote related to doing the things you told the doctor, the nutritionist, and the mental health provider during your pre-surgical preparation.

What I find humorous in this question comes from the decade of experience working with pre-ops. During these years I have heard innumerable versions of the same responses from people who are "trying to get approved for" weight loss surgery. If I could somehow collect the enthusiasm pre-ops have for (imagined, future) healthy eating, consistent exercise and enthusiasm for engaging in these behaviors, I could gather enough energy to power the world for the rest of its existence!

The reality of the follow-through of these behaviors is, well, much less enthusiastic than the words uttered before the surgery.

SO WHAT?! Who says you have to be passionate about eating healthy to do it? Who says you have to be enthusiastic about exercising to do it? What I might suggest is that you keep in mind what you ARE passionate about related to these behaviors, which is most likely the same as the reasons you had weight loss surgery in the first place. The majority of people tell me they are choosing to have weight loss surgery because they want to look and feel better about how they look, they want to improve their health andthey want to be able to do things they can't do when they are obese. THOSE are things I'm guessing YOU are passionate about.

Bottom line: If you say you want these things, that you are passionate about having these things (looking better, feeling better, improved health, and being able to do things you can't do when you are obese), then you have to be willing to do the things it takes to get that. In the case of weight loss, no matter how you slice it, losing weight and maintaining a healthy weight, requires eating healthy foods in healthy portions and exercise. You don't need to be passionate about doing those things. You just have to do them. Your passion for being able to do things you couldn't do when obese, to wear the clothes you want to wear, and to have improved health can be a large part of your motivation to follow through with those behaviors!

Cari De La Cruz & Connie Stapleton, Ph.D.

Now, please allow us to share our article: *The Medical Team Meant It. Did You?*

The Medical Team Meant It. Did You?

The Doc: Post-ops–this one's for you! (However, if you're a pre-op, you'll benefit a bunch by reading this before your procedure!) A friendly warning for everyone reading this article–pre- or post-op–these words are not for the faint of heart! You're going to be asked some questions and also asked to be 100% completely honest with yourself as you answer the questions! Don't worry too much. The questions are few in number. You don't even have to tell anybody else your answers, but if you tell yourself even a "little white lie" you'll be doing yourself a great disservice. The reason? Recovery from obesity requires being completely honest with yourself about what you are doing and what you're not doing to manage a healthy weight. Then you have to honestly decide what you are willing to do if you want what you told your weight loss surgery medical team you wanted: your health back and to be able to do things you couldn't when carrying an extra 100 + pounds.

The Post-Op: Sounds ominous, doesn't it? Just what are these questions? Can you flunk the test? The good news is, this isn't a test, but the questions can test your patience a bit, and might be challenging to answer. The goal is honesty, so just do your best and don't worry, we'll go easy on you. It won't take long to figure out that there are many more questions where these came from (and the answers will likely be the same!)

What the Nutritionist told you (and hopefully the psychologist, your PCP and the WLS surgeon, as well).

1. In some way, shape or form, during your pre-surgical preparation, the dietician told you that in order to keep your weight off over time, you are going to have to eat "healthy" portions of the right foods (and by "healthy" we do not mean "healthy" = huge; we mean "healthy" as in nutritionally healthy portions = measured/reasonable amounts of food).

Questions for you:

a. Did you get this message during your pre-surgical preparation for WLS?
b. Did you agree that you would, indeed eat "healthy" portions of food after the surgery (with an implied, forever more)?

c. Did you mean what you said when you agreed to maintaining "healthy" portions of the right foods after surgery? (I'm fairly certain you did mean it.)

d. ARE YOU DOING IT? Are you maintaining "healthy" portions of the right foods ever since you've had WLS?

e. If not, what's up???

f. If not, what are you willing to do in order to get back on track with this?

2. In some way, shape or form, during your pre-surgical preparation, the dietician told you that in order to keep your weight off over time, you need to eliminate or reduce/minimize the simple carbs that you eat (meaning white rice, white potatoes, pasta, white bread, most "baked goods," "junk food," and sugary foods (most "baked goods," candy, soda, sweet tea, cake, cookies, etc.).

Questions for you:

a. Did you get this message during your pre-surgical preparation for WLS?

b. Did you agree that you would, indeed eliminate or reduce/minimize the simple carbs that you eat (meaning white rice, white potatoes, pasta, white bread, most "baked goods," "junk food," and sugary foods (most "baked goods," candy, soda, sweet tea, cake, cookies, etc.)?

c. Did you mean what you said when you agreed to eliminate or reduce/minimize the simple carbs that you eat (meaning white rice, white potatoes, pasta, white bread, most "baked goods," "junk food," and sugary foods (most "baked goods," candy, soda, sweet tea, cake, cookies, etc.)? *(I'm fairly certain you did mean it.)*

d. ARE YOU DOING IT? Have you eliminated or reduced/minimized the simple carbs that you eat (meaning white rice, white potatoes, pasta, white bread, most "baked goods," "junk food," and sugary foods (most "baked goods," candy, soda, sweet tea, cake, cookies, etc.)ever since you've had WLS?

e. If not, what's up???

f. If not, what are you willing to do in order to get back on track with this?

What the Physician told you *(bariatric surgeon and/or PCP):*

3. It is important that you utilize the first 12–18 months (the "honeymoon period") to establish healthy lifestyle habits regarding food and exercise.

Questions for you:

a. Did you get this message during your pre-surgical preparation for WLS?
b. Did you agree that you would, indeed utilize the first 12–18 months (the "honeymoon period") to establish healthy lifestyle habits regarding food and exercise?
c. Did you mean what you said when you agreed to utilize the first 12-18 months (the "honeymoon period") to establish healthy lifestyle habits regarding food and exercise? (I'm fairly certain you did mean it.)
d. ARE YOU DOING IT? DID YOU DO IT? Are you/Did you utilize the first 12-18 months (the "honeymoon period") to establish healthy lifestyle habits regarding food and exercise?
e. If not, what's up???
f. If not, what are you willing to do in order to get back on track with this?

4. It is important that you engage in and maintain some form of physical exercise (keeping in mind your physical conditions) more days of the week than not, in order to maintain your weight loss.

Questions for you:

a. Did you get this message during your pre-surgical preparation for WLS?
b. Did you agree that you would, indeed engage in and maintain some form of physical exercise (keeping in mind your physical conditions) more days of the week than not, in order to maintain your weight loss?
c. Did you mean what you said when you agreed to engage in and maintain some form of physical exercise (keeping in mind your physical conditions) more days of the week than not, in order to maintain your weight loss? (I'm fairly certain you did mean it.)
d. ARE YOU DOING IT? Are you engaging in and maintaining some form of physical exercise (keeping in mind your physical conditions) more days of the week than not, in order to maintain your weight loss ever since you've had WLS?
e. If not, what's up???
f. If not, what are you willing to do in order to get back on track with this?

What the Psychologist/Mental Health Provider told you:

5. It is important that you fully understand that unless you do what the doctor and nutritionist tell you to do for the rest of your life, you can (and most likely will) regain your weight. Are you willing to follow through with the nutrition and exercise guidelines after surgery in order to keep the weight off? (And if you're lucky, they encouraged you to seek therapy if you struggle).

Questions for you:

a. Did you get this message during your pre-surgical preparation for WLS?
b. Did you agree that you would, indeed, do what the doctor and nutritionist told you to do for the rest of your life, or you could (and most likely would) regain your weight?
c. Did you mean what you said when you agreed to do what the doctor and nutritionist told you to do for the rest of your life, or you could (and most likely would) regain your weight? (I'm fairly certain you did mean it.)
d. ARE YOU DOING IT? DID YOU DO IT? Are you doing what the doctor and nutritionist told you to do in order to prevent regaining your weight?
e. If not, what's up???
f. If not, what are you willing to do in order to get back on track with this? ARE YOU WILLING TO GO TO THERAPY?

A Post-Op & A Doc:

Above we have noted five topics basic to nearly every surgical weight loss program in this country: 1) the need to eat healthy portions of healthy foods, 2) the need to minimize simple carbohydrates, 3) using the first year to learn and implement healthy habits, 4) engaging in, and maintaining healthy support, and 5) it is possible to regain weight after WLS if you don't follow what you were advised to do.

The Post-Op & The Doc have seventeen years collectively working in this field. We have seen and talked with thousands of patients who have shared with us that they did hear this information before surgery, they agreed to do what they learned, and they meant it. Yet many have been unable to follow through. That's normal. It's difficult to make the behavioral changes needed to keep weight off. If you start to regain, you can catch yourself and get headed in a healthy direction.

Many people are doing what it takes to get back on track so that they can get and keep their excess weight off. They do what they set out to do when they decided to have weight loss surgery: Improve their health and have the ability to do more of the things they want to do.

The best way to get into the habits needed to maintain a healthy weight or to get back on track is to use the **Gotta Do Ems**. The Gotta Do Ems are what it takes to get and keep weight off:

1. Make Healthy Food Choices
2. Maintain Portion Control
3. Exercise Regularly
4. Drink Water
5. Eat Breakfast
6. Plan Your Meals and Follow Your Plan
7. Keep a Food Diary
8. Keep an Exercise Diary
9. Use a Healthy Support System
10. Get Individual and/or Group Therapy

There are lots of excuses for not following the Gotta Do Ems. It would be easy to say that you were overwhelmed with all of the information you were given pre-surgery and couldn't possibly understand everything you agreed to. It would easy to say that you were just trying to get your forms completed so you could qualify for surgery and you therefore agreed to whatever you needed to. It would be easy to say you didn't know then what you know now, so you were committing to things you weren't prepared to honor.

Well, none of that matters because, the truth is, you can do what you said you would do and, if you really want what you say you want (improved health and a better quality of life), you must do those things you said you would.

The good news? You don't need to do them alone. In fact, as A Post-Op & A Doc always say, "No one can do this for you, but you can't do it alone." We all need support to sustain the Gotta Do 'Ems. So utilize the support offered by your medical team, your program's support group, and the people who love you and do the things you said you'd do! You'll feel great about yourself and will get the results you were looking for as you headed into weight loss surgery.

HoMeWork
by APOD

Read the article on the previous pages thoroughly and apply it to yourself. Write a few paragraphs or talk to a close friend who has been through the process of WLS, or talk to your therapist about your follow-through in comparison to what you said you would do before you had WLS. If there is a large discrepancy between what you said you would do and what you are doing, maybe it's time to re-commit to your pre-surgical resolve.

STOP

" EAT ONE, YOU'RE DONE; EAT NONE, YOU'VE WON.
DON'T START AND YOU WON'T NEED TO STOP. "

– CARI DE LA CRUZ (THE POST-OP)

Q

"I hear a lot of different people talk about what worked for them to keep their weight off after surgery. I'm so confused. I keep hearing I need to believe I can do this. The truth is that I want to do this but I'm not convinced that I really do believe in myself.

How can I increase my belief in myself?"

've been thinking about this, and while I'm sure there's stuff out there about this very thing...volumes of stuff...I'm thinking it's not in these precise words, so I'll take a stab at explaining it my way.

A lot of frustrated people ask me how I "do what I do" and how they can "do it too." In other words, they wanna know: "How can I have what you have?" WELL...The first thing to understand is, *I* didn't always have what I have. As a matter of fact, I didn't believe I could have it in the first place, so I didn't try (common theme).

What made the difference? I won't minimize the significance of weight loss surgery in my life, because it was a miracle and it did help me to change my life. BUT–it was a gift with a pretty stringent return policy, meaning that if I didn't use it, I'd lose it (no questions asked...even with a gift receipt!)

Wow. That's pretty terrifying. In those early days as a post-op, I heard people talk about "the end of the honeymoon" (like it was the end of the world) as I secretly hoped I wouldn't experience it myself. I would be the exception, I thought. I heard people talk about regain (like it was menopause or something) as I fearfully wondered if I'd be the one to escape it. Basically...I spent a lot of time focusing on what I DIDN'T want to experience. It was like I was on a bus ride and I knew that there would be roadblocks at the end of the road...right before a cliff. I didn't believe my bus had brakes, so I wouldn't be able to stop in time...I would just fly headlong into the barrier and over the cliff...and that would be the end of my weight loss journey. Imagine waking up every day wondering when the road block would finally come into view?

Clearly, being an optimist (and someone who likes to be happy and positive), this visual was disconcerting and downright yucky. Something had to change–and fast.

Enter: THERAPY. Yup. Good old-fashioned therapy. In the beginning, I wanted to focus on my weight and food addiction, but for some strange reason, we kept focusing on RELATIONSHIPS. Mostly with the people at work, and how I interacted to them. At some point, I caught on that it wasn't really about those people at all...it was about me and my relationship with MYSELF: DID I BELIEVE I COULD DO WHAT NEEDED TO BE DONE TO MAKE LIFE BETTER AT WORK–AND IN LIFE? Whoof! If that isn't the $100,000 question, I don't know what is.

And that's where my process of *Recovery From Obesity* began: I had to DECIDE that I COULD live fully and manage my weight. Did you hear that? I had to BELIEVE in what I DECIDED in order to do it. Clearly, that was the problem in the past...because, I had "decided" to do all sorts of things, but when it got right down to it–for whatever reason (because I was a perfectionist, mostly)...I didn't BELIEVE I could succeed and not surprisingly, I didn't.

But, here I was, a freaked out post-op just trying to manage my Bariatric After Life and I realized that I was faced with a very important decision. It was time to decide if I BELIEVED I was CAPABLE of living in Recovery. Uhhhh....yesss? I think I believe? I'm pretty sure. Yeah. I'm in. And, with that resounding "yes"...I was in.

Only...there was a problem. I needed to COMMIT to doing what I needed to do to get what I said I wanted (a life in Recovery From Obesity). Well...okay (I thought)...I'll commit to that.

Goodness gracious, did I ever do the Commitment Hokey Pokey! I had one hip in and one hip out...3 shrinkles in and 4 shrinkles out! I basically had alternating body parts in and others out (not always intentionally, but when you lose a lot of weight, your skin does weird things)–and it wasn't pretty.

BUT, especially when you have loose skin, playing the Hokey Pokey with COMMITMENT is not the way to solve a problem. And so, I had to take a step back (entirely out of the circle) and ponder things.

I said to myself: "I thought you'd decided that you believed you could do this. I thought you were in it to win it" Ouch. I did say that...but as it turns out, my belief was nothing more than a house of cards, which meant...I didn't really BELIEVE I could do it.

Well, I determined that this simply wouldn't stand and something would have to change. Clearly, there was something really big in the way of my Recovery: ME. YUP. I had to get out of my own way if I wanted to live FREE from the tyranny of obesity.

189

And so I did.

I DECIDED to live in Recovery.

I BELIEVED I could do it.

I COMMITTED to doing it...

I put ACTION behind it...

And...lo and behold, today I am DOING it.

You know what? My road no longer ends in a roadblock and a cliff. It's actually quite a scenic and hilly road. Indecision, Lack of Belief and Fear no longer drive my "bus" on the road of Recovery. I DO. I decided to drive my own bus and I believe I can do it, so I'm committed to holding onto that steering wheel like my life depends on it (no matter how much action I see!).

So, that's my process. It occurred to me this morning on the freeway! Just deciding to do something had never worked. Saying I was committed always failed. I would do something for awhile and stop. WHY?–Because of that critical step called BELIEF, that's why.

I had to come to the BELIEF that I could do it–and I BELIEVE that if you DECIDE to do it, you can COMMIT to being in Recovery From Obesity too.

What do you think of my process?

There are a lot of roads to Rome! I love that Cari is always willing to share her process through her *Bariatric After Life*. Her process is unique to her, although I'm sure many others, if they stopped to think about it, are going through, and have gone through, the process in a very similar way as Cari.

When I went to treatment in 1989, like most people who go to have weight loss surgery, I had no idea what I was headed for once the treatment program was over. I didn't know if I could live "forever" without chemicals to help me "calm down," (i.e., not deal with life).

Like Cari, it wasn't long into my therapy that I learned that alcohol, drugs, (or cigarettes or gambling or food or shopping) were only symptoms of the real problems, most of them involving relationships–me with myself and me with others. I was afraid that without being self-medicated in some way, I wouldn't be able to make, or have friends. I feared having to face that I had no idea how to have a healthy adult relationship with my husband. I was terrified to try to be a mother because in spite of how much I loved my children, I didn't know how to interact with them. I didn't know how to deal with my constant fear, frustration and sadness about relationships. Why? Same as most of you: I hadn't had good role models. Of course my parents loved me and my siblings. They hadn't, however, learned how to express that in healthy ways. Besides, there was addiction in my family and when that's the case, the entire family system revolves around the addict and the addiction. In essence, there was not healthy communication and there were not healthy relationships in my family. Yes, there was love. But sometimes love isn't enough...

I didn't BELIEVE I had what it took to be personally, interpersonally, or professionally successful. I hadn't learned how; I hadn't been shown how. And somewhere very deep down inside, I didn't fully believe I was capable enough (in my case, I didn't think I was smart enough) - or worthy of being successful in relationships–or in life, which is how people feel when there is any degree of neglect or abuse or addiction present in their childhood.

191

My road to Recovery, like Cari's, started with a DECISION. It was a DECISION to get help. But the decision was not based on anything remotely resembling a belief that I was worth it. My DECISION to follow through with help (I had sought counseling many times before but had quit after a few sessions), was motivated by fear of losing my husband and breaking up our family. Therefore, my DECISION was to stay in therapy, which led to treatment, which led to individual, couples and family therapy. I, and then WE, made those DECISIONS to follow through because we valued our family.

Unlike Cari, who noted BELIEF as the next step in her journey to Recovery, that was not the case for me. In fact, for me, BELIEF was the last part of the process. For me, COMMITMENT AND ACTION and a reaffirmation of my DECISION to choose Recovery, a day at a time, are what kept me on the road to living Recovery, a day at a time, for a VERY long time before BELIEF in myself even entered the picture. Sure, I had some modicum of belief in myself. But not the "I'm worth it, so I'm gonna do whatever it takes" kind of belief in myself. I believed in my husband's worth and I believed in my childrens' worth and I believed in the value of our family. I still felt pretty much like a "bad person" on the inside. I was willing to put forth EFFORT into the process toward Recovery. I was very willing to make a COMMITMENT for the sake of my FAMILY, but I didn't really believe in me.

Sometimes, we need external motivation and we need to let others believe in us until we can become willing to, and begin to, believe in ourselves. My husband and children served as external motivators for me (as perhaps they have for you in your journey toward Recovery from Obesity). I was led to an incredible therapist whom I love so very much to this day. It was baffling to me, but she seemed to see some things in me that I certainly couldn't see in myself. But I FELT her belief in me. Her belief helped fuel me and gave me sparks of insight into the abilities I have. There are times I still struggle with my BELIEF in my abilities. NOT in my belief that I am worth recovery, or my belief that I have tremendous and equal worth to every other person on the planet. But I use tools now to help me when I fall into fear or shame about myself that help me walk out of it. Primarily, I know I have made a firm COMMITMENT to Recovery, to myself, and to my husband and family AND I make use of the ACTIONS necessary to uphold those commitments.

For you, the journey to Recovery will be your own unique journey. There will most likely be the need to make DECISIONS, to develop your BELIEF in yourself, to make and re-make your COMMITMENT to health and Recovery and to follow through with ACTION. There will be many other words involved in your Recovery process, which you can identify for yourself. Whatever the specific steps, the destination is the same: Recovery from Obesity, being the person you value, living the life you value at a healthy enough weight to be able to do so!

Many Roads to Rome

There are many ingredients necessary to live in Recovery From Obesity. **Decisions, Belief, Actions,** and **Commitment** are four of them, which A Post-Op & A Doc focused on in our responses to this question. Using these four, plus any other things you feel are essential for your lifelong *Recovery From Obesity*, write about what these topics mean to you and how you do/plan to implement them in your own Recovery From Obesity.

HOME

" FOLLOW YOUR OWN YELLOW BRICK ROAD. IT'S BEEN SHOWN TO LEAD YOU HOME...THE PLACE WHERE YOU HAVE YOUR OWN RIGHT ANSWERS. "

– THE DOC

Q

" I feel like there's a food monster that's been chasing me my entire life. I heard A Post-Op & A Doc talk about this one time and you mentioned re-parenting yourself.

What's the connection and what is re-parenting?"

Before weight loss surgery, I didn't eat food...I *devoured* it. I didn't taste it; I *wolfed* it down. I didn't enjoy it; I *consumed* it like I was trying to hide the evidence. After weight loss surgery, I did the same thing–I just did it in smaller portions. And then I realized that I wasn't feeding my body. I was feeding my obsession...my addiction...the addiction I called a monster. I was being devoured by my addiction. It devoured my every waking thought and action and it was exhausting.

But, as I began to do my work in order to begin living in Recovery From Obesity–I learned that if I ever wanted to be free of its clutches, I'd have to face the food addiction "monster" head on. That was a scary proposition, trust me. But...Guess what? As I began to understand the monster, I realized it wasn't a monster at all. Oh, sure, it was ugly and frustrating and felt uncontrollable. But, far from being a monster, I learned that my addiction is really a hurt, scared, lonely, insecure child who desperately wants comfort, and the only way she knows how to get it is to eat. That child addict is me, only, I'm a grown-up now, and as a grown-up, I'm "supposed" to know better. If that's the case, how is it okay for me to let my "inner child" run the show and decide what we'll eat, how much we'll eat, and when we'll eat it? I think it isn't okay, actually, but then...

Let me take you back a few years...When I was a kid, my mom planned, prepared, portioned and served all of our meals, and she worked hard to ensure they were healthy. She didn't let us (my brother or me) eat between meals–and definitely not before dinner (lest we spoil our appetite). Once dinner was done, there were no snacks on the couch in front of the television–heck, we weren't even allowed to eat in the living room. My mom (and dad) had rules about eating that were for our benefit and we, as children, were expected to "behave" and listen. That's good parenting. Healthy boundaries, expectations and rules.

Why is it, that as a grown up, I've allowed my addicted child to run amok and not follow any rules? Clearly, running amok behavior was a recipe for disaster–one I lived daily until I decided to fully enter Recovery From Obesity AND face my Food Addiction.

The bottom line was, my addiction wasn't a monster, even though I called it a monster. Maybe it was just easier for me to call it a monster so I could justify not "controlling" it. After all, if I said it was part of myself–an "unruly" child, well, that would have made me a "bad parent" and I couldn't very well be accused of that now, could I?

Once I figured out what I was really dealing with, it was time to start parenting my own inner child and teaching her how to behave. I began by doing what any truly good, parent (who is educated about parenting) does: I tried to figure out what my child really NEEDED, NOT what she was saying she WANTED.

If you have a small child, this might be a good example for explaining this concept: Have you ever tried to have a peaceful conversation on the telephone (I mean, one that lasted longer than 5 minutes)? How'd that work out? Typically, not very well, because children like our attention and don't like when we're giving it to someone else (especially one they can't even see on the other end of a phone line)! So they do what kids do best and bug you until they get your attention–even if you're angry and yelling, it's attention, right? The sad thing is, your child is probably not being all that unreasonable. They want what every human wants: love, time, respect, comfort, YOU. Of course, in the midst of your pressing phone call, all you want is some peace and quiet and for your child to leave you alone! No problem, you issue a time-out and earn 5 minutes of uninterrupted phone time. Only, you don't get what you wanted because your child is currently throwing a tantrum, kicking the walls and waiting for you to decide that time-out is over (early).

Now imagine that child is your food addiction. **"I want you to listen to me NOW! I want! I want! I want! I want! I want! Gimme! Gimme! Gimme!"** What do you do? If you're like most addicts, you relent and say, *"What will it take to get you to shut you up? Here's a box of Girl Scout Thin Mints–now go away and leave me alone."*

But, here's the thing: Is that what the child really wanted? You gave them thin mints to keep them quiet and hopefully make them feel better… but maybe that wasn't what they needed. Maybe they were after comfort or just…quality time with you. Maybe they wanted to sit in your lap while you rubbed their hair. Maybe they needed to be heard because they'd had a bad day and no one listened to them. Maybe they wanted to play a game with you. Who knows? Certainly not you–because you just sent that food-addict-child away with a box of Thin Mints (and told her not to eat the whole thing…) Right.

Maybe you don't want to see your addiction as an inner child, maybe you can only see it as a monster, I don't know. Whatever it is, that monster or that child is DEVOURING all of your attention, which keeps you from living fully. How do I know? Well, I can't prove it scientifically, because a) I'm not a scientist, and b) I'm a terrible statistician–but I can tell you that, based upon my experience and, in checking with other recovering addicts, once you comfort the child properly–which is to say–once you figure out what you were feeding (insecurity, unworthiness, fear of not fitting in, inadequacy, not feeling loved, feeling angry and not knowing why, etc.) the child will calm down and let you have that phone conversation or eat your meal in peace.

200

When you are not trying to contend with an unruly addiction–not being DEVOURED by an endless stream of obsessive thoughts about food, weight, recipes, etc.–you can behave, think and feel like a normal person (whatever normal is). When my addiction-child was running my life, I really struggled to find peace and order in my life, but since my addiction-child is feeling (mostly) taken care of…I can think and feel and behave like a healthy adult. Oh, my child still pipes up and screams that she wants candy or cookies, but I just figure out what she is really looking for and do my best to "feed" that, instead. Or, I tell her she needs a time-out, because…she might.

This isn't easy stuff, anymore than being a parent is an easy job! It takes effort and patience and love. Yeah, love. It's not a perfect science, and sometimes we slip up. Sometimes we allow ourselves to fall back into the old behaviors of just feeding our addict-child whatever it wants so it will go away. The funny thing is, we all know how that works out, and it never ends well. Maybe it's time for you to stop abusing (neglecting, hurting, screaming at, insulting, criticizing, belittling, disliking) your addict-child and start–as The Doc would say–re-parenting them. THEY need you just as much as YOU need you.

Thoughts from a Recovering Post-Op Addict

Oh boy! This a great topic—really two topics: Food addiction and the "inner child." I'm going to do the simplest thing with the addiction part, in hopes of not starting a debate on the word "addiction," and simply say two things (which could be really simplified if I just left it at one).

But I'm not going to, so here goes.

1) If there's something you've wanted to change—really wanted to change—for a long time, and it has resulted in problems for you—and you cannot manage to change it—we're gonna consider it an addiction.

A-hem…for example: FOOD/WEIGHT! For many people, they have wanted to lose weight because they have health problems, or mobility problems, or shame problems. They have tried—repeatedly—to lose weight…and haven't been able to stop eating (too much of the wrong things). Something you've wanted to change for a long time because it's caused problems for you: *"Mr. Smith, if you don't lose weight, you're going to die from a heart attack." "Ms. Jones, if you don't lose weight soon, your foot will have to be amputated due to your diabetes." "Jim—you'd have a lot less pain in your back and could get around a lot easier if you'd lose 50 pounds." "Honey—you say you'd like to attend the kids' ball games with me but you won't because you're embarrassed about your weight. We're all suffering because I want you there, the kids want you there, and you want to be there."*

But you can't stop eating.

2) **If something causes problems for you in your life, it's a problem.** (See? I could have left it at that!) **Food** (and the consequences of too much of the wrong kinds of it) **has caused you problems.** So, food is clearly a problem. *That's what we're referring to as food addiction.*

Now on to business of the inner child and what food addiction has to do with that inner child. If you're an adult, which I assume you are since this isn't really a children's book (!), then I will assume you were once a child. Every single thought, feeling, bodily sensation and experience you had every day prior to this one, is stored in your brain. Think of them as put into file folders, maybe sorted by emotion, or grade or by year, and then stored in file cabinets. It is during your childhood years that your "default" thoughts and beliefs about the world are formed. Based on your experiences and examples, each of us comes up with our own, unique combination of beliefs and feelings about ourselves, about others and about the world.

Each of us had happy, sad, scary, lonely, embarrassing, joyful, loving, and angry times in our childhoods. Good memories. Bad memories. Each of us also had our own temperament (easy-going, anxious, etc.) and abilities for resilience (bounced back quickly, let things roll off our backs, were extremely sensitive and took things personally, extremely introverted/shy, etc.).

The combination of our temperament, resiliency levels, and experiences, and role models all contributed to how we categorized and coped with whatever took place in our lives during our childhood years. And the resulting feelings and beliefs about our experiences, as well as our youthful determination of our value/worth, or intelligence, our capabilities, etc. are stored in those file cabinets in our brains. As adults, we therefore, believe what we believe, based on this combination of factors. The more emotionally healthy the individual, the more they can handle uncertainty and ambiguity in life and the more able they are to question what they were exposed to, and change their beliefs, if their childhood "default" beliefs prove not accurate or helpful in adult life.

People who are slaves to addictions (behaviors that continually cause problems in their lives in spite of desire or previous attempts to change them), are less emotionally healthy and are not adapting their beliefs, attitudes, and behaviors based on present realities.

Befriending Your Inner Child. Inside all of us lives a younger version of us… it will serve you well to introduce yourself as an adult to yourself as a younger person. Why? Because the younger you often takes over your adult self (think about when you (still) have temper tantrums, pout, name call, "get even," or run to your room and slam the door). When you find yourself behaving like a child, take a few minutes and have a talk with the little you that is acting out. Ask her what she needs? Acknowledge that her needs are legitimate. Tell her that nothing like food or alcohol or shopping can fix what she needs (comfort, attention, affirmation, etc.) and that you are going to stay with her and she can tell you anything she wants. You may not be able to fix it, but you will listen and stay with her, not abandon her, not make fun of her, and not ignore or discount her. Tell her you can't control what other people do, and other people might do those things but you are going to stick with her because she's pretty awesome. Finally, tell her you are going to go handle whatever the issue is as an adult and will keep her with you, safe and protected. Try this… we're often trying to get our childhood needs met through others and often using childish ways. We need to acknowledge our needs and realize we can take responsibility for getting them met in healthy ways.

203

Cari De La Cruz & Connie Stapleton, Ph.D.

MONSTERS

" THERE ARE VERY FEW MONSTERS WHO
WARRANT THE FEAR WE HAVE OF THEM. "

– ANDRE GIDE

Q

"*Sometimes I get overwhelmed by all of the things to do in what A Post-Op & A Doc call 'Recovery From Obesity.' I get scared I may fail; I worry about how much weight others have lost...I compare myself. I'm scared others are talking about my current progress (or lack of it). Someone even asked me if I was afraid to succeed? Why would I want to fail on purpose? All I know is, sometimes I'm totally paralyzed by the stress!*

What can I do about this?"

was thinking about why people sometimes participate in events and why they sometimes don't. I realized that there are a lot of reasons people don't do certain things, say certain things or go certain places...Perhaps paralysis is the biggest reason of them all. It's like sometimes we're paralyzed and don't know what to do, so we do nothing. Maybe we're overwhelmed by the profundity of something we just read and are left utterly speechless (paralyzed vocal chords); maybe we just don't know how to get somewhere (paralyzed GPS)...maybe we are afraid (paralyzed with fear) so we just stay where we are.

Well, here's a little firmness for ya: **There's no room for paralysis in recovery. You MUST work it...do it...feel it. You MUST reach for it, accept it, give it.** *[Okay, MUST is a yucky word, but I kinda don't know any other word to use, except GOTTA...but we already use that for the GOTTA DO EM'S, so this is a must.]* Recovery requires your participation, not your paralysis. But, maybe you find that you don't accept support or don't participate in things because you are...PARALYZED.

PARALYSIS ANALYSIS

So, how do you recover from paralysis? Assuming it's not a permanent thing–which in emotional cases, I'd say it generally isn't–the easiest way for me to talk about overcoming paralysis is to use examples. Here are some ways that people are paralyzed and don't do or say what they need to do or say.

FEAR. This is a broad category that encompasses many, many things. So, the first thing you gotta know is, if fear is driving your bus (as The Doc says), kick it out of that driver's seat and take the wheel! You know where fear will point your bus–exactly where you DON'T want it to go. This is also called "facing your fear–and doing it anyway!" What are some things we fear?

SUCCESS, FAILURE, CRITICISM, NOT CONNECTING OR FITTING IN WITH OTHERS *(this is from a phenomenal TEDTalk)*, WHAT OTHERS THINK, THE UNKNOWN, NOT BEING PERFECT.

Oooooh. Those are just a few...but did you see something in that list that resonates with you? For me, there are a couple: PERFECTION and PEOPLE PLEASING. I was a people-pleasing-perfectionist for 40 years. Ironically, those things cannot possibly exist in harmony because there is no such thing as perfection and you can't possibly please everyone all the time. Heck, sometimes you can't please anyone any of the time! That's just reality, folks.

So, how did I recover from my paralysis of perfection and people pleasing? POSITIVE SELF-TALK. That's the answer in a nutshell. There is no magic. There is simply overwriting the negative, paralyzing recorded messages that doomed me and replacing them with powerful motivating messages that move me! This is not to say that I don't occasionally feel "THE PULL" to the negative side–because I do. The key is what I DO ABOUT IT.

When I feel paralyzed by perfection, I ask myself: *What is required of me for this project? What is expected for the completion of this project? How much time do I have? What is the best use of my time? What is the best way for me to complete this project? What will satisfy the requirements? [Believe me, as I edit and format this book, I'm asking myself all of these questions!]* When I'm finished asking myself these questions, I am always sure to remind myself that the work I've done "is sufficient" and "satisfies the requirements." I then push a little further and acknowledge the things that I've done well. I've had to teach myself that, even if I had more time to do the work "better"... there is never enough time to do it "perfectly"–and that's the key. *Can I do my best work?* Absolutely. *Can some things be better?* Probably...sometimes... but given a finite time frame, is that REASONABLE? No, so let it go. That works. I never tell myself it's "GOOD ENOUGH" because those words are poison to my brain (although they may work for you). My answer, as a recovering perfectionist to the question, "Is it good enough" will always be, "No it isn't...let me fix it." So..."THAT WORKS" is what I say to myself when I've completed a project–and then I am not paralyzed by perfection.

207

When I begin to feel paralyzed by what others think, the first thing I remind myself is this: I DO NOT KNOW WHAT THEY ARE THINKING UNLESS THEY TELL ME. Guess what? In a room full of "judgmental people"...they are not all gonna tell me. [Speaking of judgmental, I'm judgmental. You're judgmental. We are all judgmental. It's called discernment–but when it gets ugly, that's when it does the damage. I did a lot of damage by being judgmental–to myself and others. No one ever wins that game] Back to that room full of people. You walk in and people are instantly making judgments. Some are assessing you and some are putting you down. Some are thinking good things about you– and guess what? SOME AREN'T THINKING ANYTHING AT ALL ABOUT YOU. That's the key here...in reality, you're not as important as you think! What I mean is, the entire world is not thinking about you, and if they are, it's probably fleeting–until they think about someone or something else. Their thoughts don't hurt you, any more than your thoughts hurt them. If you are thinking poisonous thoughts, then it's your own thoughts hurting you. Guess what? You are thinking poisonous thoughts about yourself when you worry about what others MIGHT be thinking about you. In other words, you're poisoning yourself. A good way to get past this is to remind yourself that it's NONE OF YOUR BUSINESS. What other people think of you is NONE OF YOUR BUSINESS. Leave it alone. Drop it. Move on. Don't marinate. Don't fill in the blanks. Leave it and move on.

Good thoughts to help in your Recovery From Obesity sound like this: *"I do not know what they are thinking, and what they are thinking doesn't matter unless they are a trusted friend who wants to share their thoughts with me. Even if someone is thinking something negative about me, I won't die. Ultimately, I'm not as important to strangers and others as I want to think I am. I matter, but I'm not the center of the universe. Worrying about what others think is selfish. I cannot control what others think. Trying to manipulate their thoughts is unhealthy impression management and makes me think I have control where I don't!"*

I think that's enough for now. I'm no expert...I just know what I've learned and what works for me. Heck, it might work for you, too. But, if it doesn't...I'm okay with that. See what I did there?

Paralysis. That's not a diagnosis anyone would welcome. And yet that's exactly what it feels like at times when we are torn by dichotomous thoughts or emotions. *"I'm afraid to fail…what will others think/say?" "I'm afraid to succeed…I don't know how to live as a healthy weight person." "I think I want to go back to school so I can get a better job." "I don't think I want to put the time and energy into studying." "I want to be able to exercise so I'll feel better." "I really hate exercising so if I don't lose weight I'll have a legitimate excuse not to."*

How do you get past paralysis? The easy answer is…you move. If you move, in one direction or the other, you're in motion and can always turn around if you figure out you're moving the wrong direction. The difficult answer is…you move. It can be difficult to move, even if you start off in the wrong direction. Sometimes we need to ask for help to get going.

In the world of weight loss, this may mean asking someone to help you write a meal plan. It may mean asking someone to take an exercise class with you or go for a walk with you. It may mean asking people to keep certain foods out of the house. It may mean asking people to choose a restaurant that is not a buffet. It may mean, as Cari said, "feeling the fear and doing it anyway." You may be afraid to ask for help–do it anyway! As Cari and I have been saying for years (and you have read in this book more than a few times)–*No one can do this for you…and you can't do it alone.* Here's a simple two-step process you can try to help you get un-stuck and start moving:

1. Identify your value (as in what is important to you). If you're talking about health and weight, determine what you believe is important. For example: I value my health, which, for me, includes remaining at a healthy weight.

2. Move in the direction of your values. Using the value of health, which includes living at a healthy weight, when you feel "stuck" or "paralyzed," MOVE… and if you move in the direction of your value, then you'll be moving in the right direction! (This means if you move

209

toward being physically active, that leads to health and a healthy weight and is moving in the direction of your value. Healthy food choices would similarly be moving in the direction of your value.

Hopefully, that little bit of advice can get you moving!
As Cari wisely noted, *"There's no room for paralysis in recovery."*

210

Leave Your Mark on It

Tattoo the following words on your arm:

"Always do the next wise thing."

HEHE! I'm still waiting for someone to actually do that…but if you don't want to be the one who actually does it, just write those words down *somewhere*–actually, put them *lots of somewheres.* When you feel stuck–or even when you don't feel stuck–these words point the direction you want to move whenever you are moving!!

FEAR

" FEAR IS STATIC THAT PREVENTS
ME FROM HEARING MYSELF. "

– SAMUEL BUTLER

212

Q

" I can't stop thinking about food even though I've lost 98 pounds since surgery and am still losing. Before bed, I continue to think about what I'm going to eat when I get up. After breakfast I think about when I can have a snack and what I'll have for lunch. This goes on all day long.

How can I stop thinking about food?"

To answer this question, we're taking a trip to ancient India; please pack a *pungi* (Indian flute), some comfortable clothing, a basket and a cobra. Yes, I asked you to pack a poisonous, deadly, viper, because we're going to do a little snake charming. Never fear, once you hear my answer, I think you'll find that you've been flirting with danger for a really long time anyway, so this won't be much different.

I think we can all agree that cobras are the most dangerous when you get too close to them, so it's wise to keep a safe distance...unless you are a snake charmer, in which case, you must get close and extremely personal, flirt with a certain amount of potential disaster and continually hypnotize the snake with smooth movements–all while hoping you won't get bitten. Since you're an expert at this, you know that as long as you keep moving that flute (it's not the music, it's the movement of the flute...snakes don't have outer ears, so they can't keep the rhythm, sorry), you'll be safe from harm. The trouble comes when you (the snake charmer) forget what you're doing or just happen to zig when the snake zags. Wham! The viper strikes and you suddenly find yourself in very big trouble. This is embarrassing (to say the least), because it often happens in front of a large crowd and it's really hard to hide the fact that the snake won.

Have you figured out that the snake is a metaphor for food? Not yet? Okay, let's keep going. I told you we were taking a really long trip for this answer.

Let's say you're not a snake charmer at all; you're a food charmer, and you think that you can flirt with food and not get hurt. As long as you keep moving just right, and never take your eyes off the...what's that over there? Somebody brought red velvet cupcakes? WHAM! You just got bit by something on your plate. Actually, you bit it when you stopped paying attention to what was going on.

Sound familiar? Well, if you're anything like me, that happened a lot in your pre-surgical life as a morbidly obese person. You got "snake bit" by everything from cupcakes, to pizza, pretzels, donuts and s'mores–yet, you kept going back to that viper (food) thinking you could charm it...if you could "just...." (fill in the blank). The irony is, you always got "bit." You thought about that snake day and night...really believing you could charm it. So, why didn't you just put the lid on the basket and walk away? That's what everyone told you to do: Put the fork down and push away from the table.

Hmmm....is any of this sounding remotely familiar? Did you feel surprised when food "got you?" Did you think that having weight loss surgery would somehow make you immune to poisonous snakes?

Well, maybe that was true...for awhile. You had surgery, and...that's weird...that snake wasn't biting you anymore! Oh my gosh!!! It's charmed! It's charmed!!! You've figured this thing out! You won't get "bit" ever again! Except that....every...once...in a while...that snake you're convinced you've charmed... STRIKES OUT AT YOU, and you eat something you know you shouldn't have. Wham! It gets stuck, or you dump, or you feel guilty, so you figure that you just need to focus more on the snake (food) so it won't get you again. Before you know it, you've parked your keester in front of that snake (food) again and are focusing on it 24/7, hoping you'll be able to charm it *forever*.

Keep watching the snake (you think).

Keep watching the food (you say).

Don't take your eyes off the food (you whisper).

Ask yourself: *"Why did I have surgery?"* Did you have surgery so you could continue charming the snake (worrying about food) and not get bitten (regain weight)? If so, then you're still sitting in front of the basket and that viper (food) is still a threat. Here's a secret: As long as you focus on the snake (food), you'll have to worry about getting bitten. As long as you focus on the food, you'll have to worry about...the food.

The key to Recovery From Obesity is to figure out how to put the lid on the basket where the dangerous snake (unhealthy foods, thoughts and behaviors, mostly) is–and keep your distance. There is absolutely no reason to try to charm that snake–it's poisonous (you know that, because it probably almost killed you when you were morbidly obese). Your job is to keep away. Remember, you had surgery to live, not to flirt with disaster, and deep down inside, you know it's true, so stop focusing on the snake...the poison...the danger of it all. Stop fearing that you will get bitten if you stop thinking about the food. Give it respect (distance) and you won't have to worry about it.

215

Cari De La Cruz & Connie Stapleton, Ph.D.

There's no charming required here, just the recognition that you really can make healthy food choices by thinking of food only when you need to plan, prepare, portion and partake, and putting the lid back on the basket the rest of the time.

So, what on earth does that have to do with your question about thinking about food all the time? I dunno…it kinda sounds like you're still focused on charming that snake so you won't get "bit."

216

THE DOC SAYS

ari's answer is awesome! She totally understood this question and used an incredible analogy (as she always does, which is why I refer to her as "the word wizard")!

When I read your question, I immediately think of a question of my own, *"If you weren't thinking about food all the time, what would occupy your mind?"* My belief is that you are obsessing on food for a reason, one that is somehow protecting you.

(Note: for some people, an antidepressant medication can help with the obsessive thinking, and it may be worth talking to your physician about a medication trial. Some people have biological cases of OCD and/or anxiety and/or depression and obsessing can be symptoms.)

However, although medication can help some people sometimes, let's talk about the purpose that obsessing about food or anything else can serve in terms of a coping skill. It's often the case that at whatever point in time a person began obsessing, there were things going on in their life they didn't want to deal with.

For example, a child may become obsessed with food because his parents were fighting a lot and there was tremendous pressure in the house. Focusing on food was a way to occupy his mind and avoid fearful thoughts of whether there would be physical violence, or one of them might leave, or they might get divorced. A person may become obsessed with food if a loved one is diagnosed with a life-threatening illness. Fears about the illness may be too overwhelming, whereas thoughts of food, although annoying, are do-able.

A person may, over time, develop an obsession with food to avoid thinking about being teased, criticized, or hurt in other ways. They may continue to engage in their obsession for fear of genuine intimacy in a marriage; they stay up late at night to continue their affair with food, which can be "trusted" and "confided in," whereas their spouse might betray them if they get too close.

Obsessive thoughts of food, obsessively reading recipes and watching the food network and baking and talking about food and going out for food and looking at food, prevent one from fully living in the present; they prevent one from thinking about, feeling, and dealing with other aspects of their life that may be emotionally troublesome for them. Recovery From Obesity requires more than simply getting one's consumption of food managed. Recovery From Obesity requires looking at the role that your relationship with food plays in your life and what it prevents you from experiencing.

218

Food For Thought

1. Think back to how long you have obsessed about food.

2. Ask yourself if you obsessed about anything before you obsessed about food.

3. Think about what was going on in your world when you can first remember obsessing about food or anything else.

4. Make time to give some thought to what was happening in life at that time.

5. Talk about, write about, draw pictures about what you were thinking, feeling, and experiencing at that time.

6. Get professional help if necessary.

7. Refuse to engage in food porn. Deal with life…whatever is going on in life. Deal with it in the moment. Talk to others about your feelings. Learn positive, healthy coping skills.

Cari De La Cruz & Connie Stapleton, Ph.D.

LIVE

" YOU CAN'T THINK YOUR WAY INTO A NEW WAY
OF LIVING; YOU HAVE TO LIVE YOUR WAY INTO A
NEW WAY OF THINKING. "

– RECOVERY SLOGAN

Q

A Post-Op & A Doc asked our online friends on Facebook a few questions and many of you provided us with some insightful answers. Your feedback was so good, in fact, we decided to include the conversation here!

First, read each question and set of answers and see if you can relate to any of the responses; then, read our thoughts* about it.

*We didn't say 'read our minds' as that's not the goal of recovery.

1. EMOTIONS–When I think about food, I feel _____:

- *Overwhelmed/trapped.*

- *Challenged! To meet my food addiction head on! Sometimes I win, sometimes it does. Thankfully I win more often than not!*

- *In all honesty, very happy!*

- *Gross...I don't like food, so I have to force myself to eat.*

- *Annoyed. Annoyed that what is healthy for us costs a lot more than what is bad for us. Annoyed that I have severe allergies to many healthy foods. On the bright side—there's always a bright side—I know there are healthy alternatives to the healthy alternative I cannot have.*

- *Frightened .*

- *I'm scared. It came out of nowhere.*

- *Guilty.*

- *Depressed....wishing all the really healthy foods didn't cost so much!!*

- *Empowered, because I know I will never eat like I used to. I'm eating to live, not living to eat anymore.*

- *Anxious.*

- *Apathetic.*

- *Detached.*

- *Boxed in.*

- *Inspired.*

- *Bored.*

- *Frustrated.*

222

- *Lost.*

- *Liberated.*

- *Fat.*

- *I seriously hate food; I have to force myself to eat, I see food as my biggest enemy.*

- *Like it will fill the gap.*

- *Helpless.*

- *That my drama is over with food since my sleeve.*

- *It's a friend AND a foe but I guess that's not an EMOTION. I guess my feeling would be FEAR.*

- *That it no longer controls me, I control it!*

- *Sometimes very angry because I am addicted to food and I have to watch everything that goes in my mouth; other times helpless and hopeless…less now with the Band…but still, sometimes.*

THE BUS

" DON'T LET FEELINGS DRIVE YOUR BUS. (BUT DON'T STUFF THEM IN THE BACK, EITHER!) "

– A POST-OP & A DOC

You Answered...

2. **Since losing weight, I feel _____:**

- *Some positive and some not so positive things. Healthier, more comfortable in my clothes, no longer scared I won't fit in a chair, more agile. I also feel uneasy when people comment/notice, I feel more insecure about my food choices (no idea why), and actually feel fatter(???). Go figure. It's a journey–a process. It'll balance out.*

- *Energetic!!*

- *Fantastic!*

- *It makes me feel really good. But I do still "feel" the same size I used to be–or worse!*

- *Kind of strange, if I'm being honest...I have never been this small and for me, I think I had gotten so used to living in my bigger body and functioning in the world that way...with the way people treat you and how you have to make certain adjustments because of your size–that for me is very strange and odd to now live as a smaller person and shop in any store that I want and fit into restaurant booths. The way that people treat me is different–even the people that knew me before my surgery. I have a hard time figuring out how to make this new body work and what all it can do. To me I am the exact same person as I was when I was bigger, but every day I kind of find new reasons why everything is different–and it feels very strange.*

- *Lighter! In many ways.*

- *More optimistic, excited for opportunities, more attractive, in control. However...I am still the same; same demons, same flaws, same negative thoughts at times...*

- *Scared of losing what I have. For many areas if my life, not just my size, the more I have of what I want, the more I know how painful it would be to lose it, or in this case gain it. Things like being healthy and fit...in this instance. Perhaps my commitment to being healthy and fit. Just knowing that it is not easy and never will be. Do/will I continue to be diligent and on top of it all? There is a lot to lose when you have a lot.*

- *Really good and healthy BUT I think I'm also terrified of gaining any back and I do feel 'fatter' now. My clothes are tighter because I always wore everything so loose.*

- *More self-conscious of my body.*

- *I feel free, but only after I did the self-work and therapy to work through and process all the things that led me to overeat and become obese.*

- *Energized beyond description.*

- *On the positive side, I feel accomplished. On the negative side, I am miserable, more unhappy than pre-weight loss, but perhaps that's because I am facing my feelings instead of drowning them.*

- *Befuddled.*

- *I feel stressed. I lost over 50 pounds. And maintained it for well over two years. Recently, (the last few months) it has been sneaking up on me even though I have not really changed the way I eat. Maybe I am a little less active then I was during the summer but I really do not know what is going on. I just hope it stops soon...I kinda like my wardrobe just the way it is.*

- *I feel vain. Like I always want to be looking in the mirror. But also I still feel really fat. Doesn't make much sense as it seems a bit contradictory.*

- *Grief at losing my wardrobe. I've always worn baggy, loose clothing, but pants and tops are even baggier and looser than ever. When I went to work one day last week, my boss jokingly asked if I was wearing loungewear. I do not want to invest in any new clothes right now.*

FACT CHECK

FEELINGS AREN'T FACTS. WHEN YOUR FEELINGS GET 'TOO BIG,' ADD A LITTLE "FACT" TO THE EQUATION.

– THE DOC

3. I'm afraid I won't be able to give up _____ after WLS.

- I was afraid I wouldn't be able *to give up the anonymity that being fat provided me with. I've discovered that it's a work in progress. I've had to allow myself permission to be seen and heard, and with support I am slowly realizing that what I have to say is important.*

- *I was honestly afraid I wouldn't be able to give up "favorite" foods. Do I still want them? Sure, from to time. But, not giving in...well, it's not so hard when my mind is in the game.*

- *Carbs, and I did for awhile, struggling now.*

- *Chocolate and peanut butter sundae. Every year for 2 years after surgery I would try to eat some of a sundae when the ice cream shop opened in the summer. I got so sick both times it killed my craving.*

- *Diet Dr. Pepper. And yes, I have (given it up) and now I can sleep all night without having to get up and go to the restroom.*

- *Trying not to be too dramatic but as usual the drama queen has to say that I feared I would not be able to give up my 'padded cell' of fat. It protected me from others and me from myself—if that makes sense. I'm at war with myself right now with it because I am still in the middle of getting rid of it. I'm talking in circles but it makes sense in my head. I'm losing my protection.*

- *Diet cola was my last hold-out before surgery, I drank it up until the day I started my pre-op liquid diet. I'm 2 and a half months out from surgery now and have thought of it on about 3 occasions but know it is not something I can reasonably attempt! And I'm surviving fine without it.*

- *I was afraid I wouldn't be able to binge anymore. Weird right? That's how I dealt with my issues. Now I have to be still and turn to other things instead of food. I'm still figuring it out but I'm not bingeing.*

- *I miss not cleaning my plate and everyone's around me! I always thought it was a sin to waste food. I really don't miss it since surgery. My small pouch of a stomach let's me know when I've had enough. The rest? Right into the garbage disposal.*

- *Soda. It's crazy because for years I only drank lemonade and fruit punch. They told me I couldn't have soda and I started binging on it for a month. Crazy because it was so mental for me. Tell me I can't have something and I want it. The outcome was good though. Went on my two week liquid diet with no soda and haven't looked back since.*

ACTION

" YOUR ACTIONS FOLLOW THE DIRECTION OF YOUR
MOST DOMINANT THOUGHT. TO GET WHERE YOU
WANT TO GO, FOCUS ON WHO YOU WANT TO BE. "

– THE DOC

THE POST-OP SAYS

As usual, I noticed that your responses to the first two questions pretty much fit into one of four sections: FEARFUL, FAILING, HOPEFUL and HEALING. Wanna see?

How you feel about food.

HOPEFUL	HEALING
HAPPY! EMPOWERED. LIBERATED. THE FOOD DRAMA IS OVER. INSPIRED. I'M IN CONTROL.	ANNOYED... BUT LOOKING ON THE BRIGHT SIDE. CHALLENGED; I WIN MORE TIMES THAN MY ADDICTION.

— When I think about food, I feel... —

FEARFUL	FAILING
TRAPPED. ANXIOUS OVERWHELMED. BOXED IN. HOPELESS. FRIGHTENED. SCARED. AFRAID.	HELPLESS. GROSS. GUILTY. BORED. LOST. FAT. HELPLESS. DEPRESSED. FRUSTRATED APATHETIC. FOOD IS MY ENEMY DETACHED. DEPRESSED.

How you feel since losing weight.

HOPEFUL

ENERGETIC!

NO LONGER SCARED.

FANTASTIC!

REALLY GOOD.

FREE!

LIGHTER

IN CONTROL.   (IN MANY WAYS!)

EXCITED FOR   MORE
OPPORTUNITIES   ATTRACTIVE.

ACCOMPLISHED.

HEALING

SOME POSITIVE;
SOME NEGATIVE,
BUT HEALTHIER.

COMFORTABLE
IN MY CLOTHES.

IT WILL
BALANCE
OUT.

STRANGE, BUT
ADJUSTING.

DILIGENT.

AGILE.

— Since losing weight, I feel... —

UNEASY.

INSECURE.

SELF-CONSCIOUS.

TERRIFIED.

SCARED OF
LOSING WHAT
I HAVE.

SCARED.

AFRAID.

FEARFUL

WORSE.   VAIN & FAT.

FATTER.

SAME DEMONS
SAME FLAWS.

MIERSABLE.   .SAME NEGATIVES

STRESSED FROM

UNHAPPY.   REGAIN.

BEPUDDLED.

FAILING

What do you notice about question one? Most of your feelings still revolve around fear and failure! What that tells me is, there's a lot of "Stinkin' Thinkin'" going on and not enough positive self-talk! Fortunately, you can fix that -- but it's gonna take more than a firm talking to! You'll have to put some action behind those positive new thoughts. Now, the third question revolved around "fear of loss" - in other words, what you were afraid of giving up (losing). Most of your answers pertained to food (coincidence? I think not! Especially when you've been putting all of your emotional eggs into one food basket for a very long time!), but a couple of you mentioned physical traits: Anonymity and Protection. In speaking with lots of post-ops through the years, I have learned that this is not uncommon, although it wasn't my experience because when I was obese, I felt vulnerable and anything BUT anonymous. In my case, I felt like I couldn't hide if I tried (mostly from myself) and didn't have a voice worth hearing anyway (which, unsurprisingly, didn't stop me from talking!)

I guess if I were going to tie this all up in a big, Barbie Pink bow, I'd say: I think all of our "fears of loss" begin with a kernel of truth and then take on a life of their own until they become, well...bigger than life itself! As we become more and more obese, we unwittingly feed our fears with food, which gives them more power than they deserve, and then (ironically) we fear losing the very things that made us so unhappy and afraid!

Here's the good news: Most (if not all) of those fears weren't as big as you believed, and you've gained unbelievable strength from knowing you really can live with the loss. I'll leave you with this: As you look at those graphics showing your thoughts about HOPE, HEALING, FEAR and FAILURE, do you see any *negative* things you can LOSE? How about some *positive* things you can GAIN? If you can't see either, you might want to go back and reread this book; I'm betting *something* will jump out at you.

THE DOC SAYS

Wow! What an amazing variety of responses! And none of them are "right" or "wrong." Feelings are neither right nor wrong; they just are. The thing about them is…we don't want them to drive the bus. *WHAT?*

I often talk about not letting feelings drive the bus. What that means is not to let how you feel dictate what you do. Think about it…people very often let feelings drive the bus and let's look at what happens:

- a man and woman (both married) meet at work and develop a friendship and before long they are confusing their friendship for romantic feelings; they end up in a compromising position and talk about how "happy" they feel when they are together and how "wonderful" they feel and reason that if they feel so "happy and wonderful" when they're together, how can it possibly be wrong… (you know how this story ends)

- a woman gets upset at work because she put a great deal of time and effort into a project; the boss gives her a list of ten things that need to be "fixed" and the woman goes home and takes out her anger on her husband and children (not a happy scene)

- a young man feels betrayed by his girlfriend when he sees her talking to another guy on campus; he gets in his car and lets his anger "drive" – way too fast, which lands him a whopping speeding ticket

You get the idea. Our feelings, if we allow them to dictate our behavior, can lead to trouble. It's the same with feelings regarding food. If we're feeling "great," we sometimes give ourselves an excuse to "celebrate" with food "just this once." If we're feeling horrible about food, we can easily fall into the "why bother" pit.

The "take home" message is this: no matter how you feel, ALWAYS DO THE NEXT WISE THING, whether it's about food or any other aspect of your life!

Make sticky notes and place them where you need them. Write on them: *"Given my past experiences, my current circumstances, and my hopes and dreams for the future, what is the wise thing to do in this situation?"*

232

SUPPORT

" YOU CAN'T DO IT ALONE,
BUT NO ONE CAN
DO IT FOR YOU. "

— A POST-OP & A DOC

Cari De La Cruz & Connie Stapleton, Ph.D.

RECOVERY

The Post-Op Says...

My grandpa was an alcoholic. When he died, he had more than 20 years sober and was a sponsor to many. Being so involved in Alcoholics Anonymous, there were lots of AA sayings around the house, including a rainbow sticker on his car bumper that said, *"Easy Does It"* and one on the steering wheel that said *"One Day At A Time."* Now, at age 8, I didn't get it. I figured the only way to do *anything* was "one day at a time" (duh) and why would you need a sticker to remind people not to speed? Weird. He also had framed copies of the *Serenity Prayer* in each bathroom, a "Big Book" on his nightstand, and—oh yeah—**a fully stocked liquor cabinet above the fridge**. For years, that last part is what confused me the most about alcoholism, addiction and recovery. How could an alcoholic keep booze in the house and offer *everybody* drinks—including me? When I was 9, I actually took him up on the deal and said yes to a "7-and-7" (which he said was 7-Up and some other "7.") Either he was a lousy bartender, or he purposely made that drink more "7" than "7" because, it was terrible! Yuck! Alcohol tasted disgusting—which was good news because, I was convinced that meant I could never become addicted.

Thus, began my (mis)understanding of addiction.

Which brings me to this book and my own recovery. The Doc talks about addiction being a family disease. Well, she's right—but it wasn't just my grandpa; it was people in my own house (who shall remain nameless because one of them might be reading this book). Food was the drug of choice when things got stressful so, once I grew into a tortured, overly dramatic, stressed-out teen, I knew right where to turn for comfort: FOOD. Unfortunately, once I started, I *didn't* stop—because I *couldn't* stop, and I soon felt worthless, ashamed and hopeless. My misunderstood addiction eventually weighed 320 pounds and wore size 28/30 pants. Food had become a very BIG PROBLEM and by the time I had surgery, I was a full-blown food addict—which was a surprise, because no one ever told me you could be addicted to something you need to live.

This all sounds confusing, because I had surgery to lose weight and cure my obesity. I never thought I'd have to deal with some sort of addiction two years down the road, but after losing half my body weight, all I had to show for it was a size "S" t-shirt, a bunch of shrinkles and an insatiable desire to eat. They say, "Wherever you go, there you are"...Well, I was right where I left me...and boy, was I hungry.

234

Fortunately, that's not the end of this story; it's actually the beginning. Thanks (in no small part) to a few compassionate and brave therapists, some reasearch, reading, and a willingness to accept that my problem was bigger than me, I can joyfully say that **I've learned what it means to live fully in Recovery From Obesity**. I have learned that I must be aware of my thoughts, feelings and behaviors, own my crap, apologize when I am wrong, take responsibility for my behavior–you know, follow the Recipe For Recovery that we always talk about–one day at a time–for a lifetime. Oh, and I also learned that I had to make a list (fondly called "**THE LIST**"): A physical (typed) inventory of my trigger foods–the things I can't start (because I won't stop), the things I hide or feel guilty about eating; the things I'll eat–whether I'm hungry or not; the things I won't share, can't ignore and regret far more than I enjoy. It's a pretty "exhaustive" list, and man, is it scary–which might be why it took me so long to write it. I was terrified that I wouldn't be able to live without **THE THINGS ON THE LIST**. But, one day, I decided I was more afraid to live *with* those foods than I was to live *without* them...and the list was born.

Since that day, I've steered clear of those things. Sure, I want them sometimes, but I want Recovery more; so, when I'm faced with something on my list, I simply say, "Nope. It's on the list" or "that's not an option," and I move on. I have learned that the temporary high I feel from eating junk, pales in comparison to the unbearable low I feel when I'm done. I continue to add things to the list if they become a problem and–guess what?–I continue to live. But, that's not the end of my story...

Here's what I didn't say in my acknowledgment: I owe the very substance and strength of my recovery to one person–who just so happens to be the other half of this duo: **Connie Stapleton**. In her firm, fair, loving way, she has taught me what recovery means, teaching me how to forgive, get over, give credit to, and actually enjoy *myself*. She has encouraged me to finish what I start and helped me see that I really can do the things I spent a lifetime telling myself I couldn't. She laughs at (most of) my jokes, isn't bothered when I talk while I pack, irons my clothing when we travel (even though she hates it–ironing–not my clothing) and enjoys my creations. She's helped me see that it's not all about me and shown me the freedom that can only come from living fully in recovery. Oh, and she has great shoes. I thank God everyday for His wisdom in bringing us together. Friend, my cup joyfully runneth over...*I love and thank you.*

That's my Recovery journey so far. I don't know what tomorrow will bring but I know it will take care of itself. I truly hope that if you see yourself in any of these words, you will seek help and choose Recovery...just as I did.

I believe you can do it.

Cari De La Cruz & Connie Stapleton, Ph.D.

RECOVERY

The Doc Says...

Recovery has been a way of life for me for the past 25 years. I was 16 when I took my first drink. This was not the first way I had found to distance myself from my feelings, but it was the quickest and most effective way I had discovered. Alcohol, and a vicious eating disorder "served" me all through college and helping me to avoid the loneliness that enveloped me there, helped me avoid the reality that my parents were in the process of divorcing and my four younger siblings were living at home. After I graduated and got married, I found codeine, which was much easier for a career woman and mother of small children to hide. Addiction being what it is—a disease of disaster—led to my personal disasters and I entered an outpatient treatment program in May of 1989.

Since learning to deal with life on it's terms (meaning to deal with things as they happen), I and my family have experienced a kind of joy that is indescribable. Of course life is life and there are stressors, frustrations, difficult situations and problems of all sorts. But there is no alcohol, no drugs, no food, no nothing to interfere with our relationships, to take our attention away from experiencing life wholeheartedly. In Recovery, my husband and I learned to parent better, to communicate better, to enjoy the present better, and to love one another and others better.

Recovery IS our way of life. It happens a day at a time. Life is such an adventure and so much of what we make it! I have friends in Recovery like I had never known before...friends to confide in with confidence. Friends who are willing to set me straight when need be. My husband and I have been married for 30+ years. Our children are happy adults starting their own families. We have grandbabies, which is a gift like no other. We LIKE each other and spend a great deal of time together. This would not be the case if we had not CHOSEN Recovery—and put forth the effort, adopted the attitude, and walked the walk that living fully in Recovery requires. It's worth it—and then some!

My hope is that each of you will choose Recovery and will experience the kind of joy that really cannot be put into words.

Choose to experience it!

If you want what you say you want, you gotta do what you gotta do.

Gotta Do, Em's™

1. **Make Healthy Food Choices.**

"EAT HEALTHY FOODS & ENJOY BETTER MOODS."

2. **Maintain Portion Control.**

"SIZE MATTERS. WEIGH IT. COUNT IT. MEASURE IT. OWN IT."

3. **Exercise Regularly.**

"IF YOU MOVE IT YOUR JEANS WILL PROVE IT."

4. **Drink Water All Day.**

TODAY'S MENU
☑ Breakfast
☐ Lunch
☐ Snack
☐ Dinner

"IF YOU'RE NOT GOING THE WATER'S NOT FLOWIN'."

5. **Eat Breakfast.**

"START YOUR DAY WITH A BITE & YOU'LL END YOUR NIGHT RIGHT."

237

6. **Plan Your Meals & Follow Your Plan.**

"DON'T LEAVE IT TO FATE; PLAN WHAT'S ON YOUR PLATE."

7. **Keep A Food Diary.**

"WRITE IT DOWN & IT WON'T WEIGH YOU DOWN."

8. **Keep An Exercise Diary.**

"JOT WHEN YOU TROT & KEEP A LOG OF YOUR JOG."

9. **Get Enough Sleep.**

"DO IT RIGHT...SLEEP TIGHT EVERY NIGHT."

10. **Use A Healthy Support System.**

"LEND A HAND & GET SOME HELP. WHEN YOU SHARE YOUR HEART, YOU KEEP YOUR HEALTH."

11. **Get Individual and/or Group Therapy.**

"LIFE IS HARD & YOU FEEL HURT. FIND A DOC & DO THE WORK."

Cari De La Cruz & Connie Stapleton, Ph.D.

Give It Away

We shared our answers to your *"whys?"* – now,
share this book and help others get *"wise."*

Questions?

Send us your questions so we can get started on
Straight Talk With A Post-Op & A Doc, Volume 2!

Contact Us

www.conniestapletonphd.com/apod
facebook.com/apostopandadoc
twitter.com/apostopandadoc
thepostop@apostopandadoc.com
thedoc@apostopandadoc.com

~~The End.~~

The Beginning

Made in the USA
Charleston, SC
05 October 2015